First World War
and Army of Occupation
War Diary
France, Belgium and Germany

28 DIVISION
84 Infantry Brigade
Welsh Regiment
1/6th Battalion.
23 October 1914 - 31 October 1915

WO95/2277/5

The Naval & Military Press Ltd
www.nmarchive.com
Published in association with The National Archives

Published by

The Naval & Military Press Ltd

Unit 10 Ridgewood Industrial Park,

Uckfield, East Sussex,

TN22 5QE England

Tel: +44 (0) 1825 749494

www.naval-military-press.com

www.nmarchive.com

This diary has been reprinted in facsimile from the original. Any imperfections are inevitably reproduced and the quality may fall short of modern type and cartographic standards.

© **Crown Copyright**
Images reproduced by permission of The National Archives, London, England, 2015.

Contents

Document type	Place/Title	Date From	Date To
Heading	1st Battalion Suffolk Reg Oct 1914-Oct 1915.		
Heading	28th Division 84th Infy Bde 1st Bn Suffolk Regt Oct 1914-Oct 1915 To Salonika		
Heading	84th Bde. 28th Div. War Diary. 1st Suffolk Regiment. 23rd October 1914 to 31st January 1915. Attached:- Appendices 1-7.		
Heading	War Diary.		
War Diary	Liverpool	23/10/1914	23/10/1914
War Diary	Lichfield	23/10/1914	17/11/1914
War Diary	Felixstowe	17/11/1914	17/11/1914
War Diary	Hursley Park	07/12/1914	07/12/1914
War Diary	Winchester	04/01/1915	16/01/1915
War Diary	Southampton	16/01/1915	16/01/1915
War Diary	S.S. Mount Temple	17/01/1915	18/01/1915
War Diary	Havre	19/01/1915	19/01/1915
War Diary	Rouen	19/01/1915	19/01/1915
War Diary	Hazebrouck	20/01/1915	20/01/1915
War Diary	Merris	20/01/1915	31/01/1915
Heading	Appendix 1.		
Miscellaneous	84th Infantry Brigade Order for March and Embarkation, 16th January. Appendix No 1.	15/01/1915	15/01/1915
Miscellaneous	To 1st Suff R.	15/01/1915	15/01/1915
Miscellaneous	BM 376	15/01/1915	15/01/1915
Miscellaneous	Secret.		
Miscellaneous	28th Division Orders for Embarkation.	15/01/1915	15/01/1915
Miscellaneous	March and Embarkation Table for Saturday, 16th January.	16/01/1915	16/01/1915
Miscellaneous	Appendix		
Heading	Appendix 2.		
Miscellaneous	A Copy Issued to Each O.C. Unit. Appendix No 2.	13/01/1915	13/01/1915
Heading	Appendix 3.		
Miscellaneous	Notes on Trenches. Appendix No. 3.		
Heading	Appendix 4.		
Miscellaneous	Appendix No 4		
Heading	Appendix 5.		
Miscellaneous	Appendix No 5.		
Heading	Appendix 6.		
Miscellaneous	Eighty Fourth Bde. Appendix No. 6.	18/02/1915	18/02/1915
Miscellaneous	SK 145 S. 4th Bde.	18/02/1915	18/02/1915
Heading	Appendix 7.		
Miscellaneous	84th Bde. Appendix No. 7.	22/02/1915	22/02/1915
Heading	84th Bde. 28th Div. Battalion went with Bde to 5th Div, 22.2.15 War Diary. 1st Suffolk Regiment. February. 1915.		
War Diary	Merris	01/02/1915	02/02/1915
War Diary	Ypres	03/02/1915	04/02/1915
War Diary	Blauwe Port Farm	05/02/1915	05/02/1915
War Diary	Verbranden Molen Farm	05/02/1915	07/02/1915
War Diary	Ypres	07/02/1915	09/02/1915
War Diary	Verbranden Molen	09/02/1915	10/02/1915

War Diary	Ypres	10/02/1915	11/02/1915
War Diary	Nr Ouderdom	12/02/1915	12/02/1915
War Diary	Billets Nr Ouderdom	12/02/1915	15/02/1915
War Diary	Ypres	15/02/1915	18/02/1915
War Diary	Kruistrat	18/02/1915	23/02/1915
War Diary	Bailleul	24/02/1915	27/02/1915
War Diary	Bus Farm	28/02/1915	28/02/1915
Heading	84th Bde. 5th Div. War Diary. 1st Suffolk Regt. March 1915. Attached:- Operation Orders.		
War Diary	Busfarm	01/03/1915	04/03/1915
War Diary	In Trenches	05/03/1915	07/03/1915
War Diary	Bailleul	08/03/1915	14/03/1915
War Diary	Near Ploegsteert	14/03/1915	15/03/1915
War Diary	Trenches	16/03/1915	16/03/1915
War Diary	St Patricks Day	17/03/1915	18/03/1915
War Diary	Bailleul	18/03/1915	21/03/1915
War Diary	Dranoutre	22/03/1915	25/03/1915
War Diary	Trenches	26/03/1915	28/03/1915
War Diary	Dranoutre	29/03/1915	31/03/1915
Heading	Operation Orders.		
Operation(al) Order(s)	1st Suffolk Regt. Operation Order No. 2.	25/03/1915	25/03/1915
Operation(al) Order(s)	1st Suffolk Regt. Operation Order No. 3.	26/03/1915	26/03/1915
Operation(al) Order(s)	1st Suffolk Regt. Operation Order No. 4.	27/03/1915	27/03/1915
Operation(al) Order(s)	1st Suffolk Regt. Operation Order No. 5.	01/04/1915	01/04/1915
Heading	28th Division. 84th Brigade. The 84th Bde required 28th Div from 5th Division-6/4/15. War Diary 1st Suffolk Regt. 1st-9th April 1915.		
War Diary	Billets Near Dranoutre.	01/04/1915	09/04/1915
Heading	28th Division. 84th Brigade. War Diary 1st Suffolk Regt. 9th-31st May 1915.		
War Diary		09/05/1915	24/05/1915
War Diary	In the Field	24/05/1915	25/05/1915
War Diary		24/05/1915	26/05/1915
War Diary		26/05/1915	31/05/1915
Miscellaneous	A Form. Messages And Signals		
Miscellaneous	A Form. Messages And Signals.		
Miscellaneous	To Bde Maj 84th Bde.		
Miscellaneous	A Form. Messages And Signals.		
Miscellaneous			
Miscellaneous	A Form. Messages And Signals.		
Heading	28th Division. 84th Brigade. War Diary 1st Suffolk Regt. June 1915.		
War Diary		01/06/1915	30/06/1915
Heading	28th Division. 84th Brigade. War Diary 1st Suffolk Regt. July 1915.		
War Diary		01/07/1915	31/07/1915
Heading	28th Division. 84th Brigade. War Diary 1st Suffolk Regt. August 1915.		
War Diary	Arcadia Dug-Outs	01/08/1915	31/08/1915
Heading	84th Bde. 28th Div. 1st Suffolks September 1915.		
Miscellaneous	On His Majesty's Service.		
War Diary		01/09/1915	30/09/1915
Heading	84th Bde. 28th Div. Embarked with Bde for Salonika 24.11.15. 1st Suffolks October 1915.		
Miscellaneous	On His Majesty's Service.		
War Diary		01/10/1915	31/10/1915

1st BATTALION SUFFOLK REG

OCT 1914 - OCT 1915

28TH DIVISION
84TH INFY BDE

1ST BN SUFFOLK REGT
OCT 1914 - OCT 1915

To SALONIKA

84th Bde.
28th Div.

WAR DIARY.

1st SUFFOLK REGIMENT.

23rd OCTOBER 1914
TO
31st JANUARY 1915.

Attached:-

Appendices 1 - 7.

WAR DIARY.

Army Form C. 2118.

WAR DIARY
or
INTELLIGENCE SUMMARY
(Erase heading not required.)

Instructions regarding War Diaries and Intelligence Summaries are contained in F.S. Regs., Part II. and the Staff Manual respectively. Title pages will be prepared in manuscript.

Hour, Date, Place	Summary of Events and Information	Remarks and references to Appendices
LIVERPOOL OCT 23rd 1914 10 AM	Disembarked from H.T. GRANTULLY CASTLE and proceeded in two trains to LICHFIELD STAFFS where the Battalion was accommodated in Huts. Whittington Barracks & Rem proceeded on 3 days leave. Out Battalion started to discharge a Certain number of Men being engaged in drawing 14 days leave.	B3
LICHFIELD OCT 23rd – NOV 17th		B1
FELIXSTOWE NOV 17th 3 PM	Arrived at Felixstowe and accommodated in billets. Limited stores received including 15 tons transport.	B1
HURSLEY PARK DEC 7th 3 PM	Arrived WINCHESTER by rail & proceeded to HURSLEY PARK and accommodated in tents. Mobilization proceeded, took drafts from 3rd Battalion Suffolk Regt. Arrived no 225 strong, out no 40 strong. Had one Inspection Carried out. Camp a Sea of mud. pitched tents for remainder of 84th Inf Bde = 8th Inf Bde 28th Division.	B1
WINCHESTER JAN 4th 1915	Owing to the extremely bad weather all tents were battened. Billets at WINCHESTER when Mobilization was completed a Furlers draft of 30 men received from 3rd Batt Suffolk Regt.	B1
JAN 5th	2 Lieut Puckhabu & 2 Lieut Payns 3rd Batt. Suffolk Regt arrived to take on details. Mobilization completed. Capt Applied proceeded to Advance party to HAVRE as a communication officer on the 11th Jan. Horsetoad & 6 NCOs & Men advance Billeting party left WINCHESTER to FRANCE 12 NOON JAN 15th	B.
JAN 16th 8.50 AM	Paraded strength 26 officers 996 other ranks & proceeded by Route March to BRYNER & SOUTHAMPTON to embark for FRANCE.	B3. See appendix No 1.

Army Form C. 2118.

WAR DIARY
or
INTELLIGENCE SUMMARY

(Erase heading not required.)

Instructions regarding War Diaries and Intelligence Summaries are contained in F. S. Regs., Part II. and the Staff Manual respectively. Title pages will be prepared in manuscript.

Hour, Date, Place	Summary of Events and Information	Remarks and references to Appendices
SOUTHAMPTON JAN 16TH 1.30 P.M.	Arrived Southampton Docks. R.O counter on the hand.	B
" " 2.0 P.M.	Started embarkation on S.S. MOUNT TEMPLE	
" " 4.0 P.M.	Completed embarkation	B
" " 5.0 P.M.	Sailed with Head Quarters of 84TH INF BDE + 103RD Battery R.F.A on board, + proceeded to ST HELENS ISLE OF WIGHT. anchored.	B
S.S. MOUNT TEMPLE JAN 17TH 5 P.M.	Sailed under escort of destroyers	
" " 12 M.N.	arrived off HAVRE	
" " JAN 18TH 9 A.M.	entered HAVRE HARBOUR	B
" " 1.30 P.M.	Started disembarkation	
" " 4.30 P.M.	Completed disembarkation	
HAVRE JAN 19TH 2.30 A.M.	Started entraining	
" " 6.30 A.M.	Completed entraining + left HAVRE in one train except two platoon + A Coy (Lt BRADLEY + 56 all ranks + 102 other ranks) who entrained in a train leaving HAVRE at 8 A.M. Two men a Coy left behind at HAVRE sick	B See appendix No 2.
ROUEN JAN 19TH 9.30 A.M.	Arrived and left at 9.50 A.M. 2 M.S. Cate (O.R.S) left here to join A.G's office	
HAZEBROUCK JAN 20TH 3.30 A.M.	Arrived. Completed detraining at 6.30 A.M. Lt Bradleys Party reported.	B
MERRIS JAN 20TH 10 A.M.	Arrived by March Route + went into Billets. Lieut O.I. Wade + 6 N.C.O.s + men reported. Protection arranged for by sending a Rests to front + flanks of Billets	
" JAN 21ST	Settled in Billets. Lieut F.O.C. Hunt admitted hospital sick	B

1247 W 8299 200,000 (E) 8/14 J.B.C. & A.   Forms/C. 2118/11.

WAR DIARY or INTELLIGENCE SUMMARY

Army Form C. 2118.

(Erase heading not required.)

Instructions regarding War Diaries and Intelligence Summaries are contained in F. S. Regs., Part II. and the Staff Manual respectively. Title pages will be prepared in manuscript.

Hour, Date, Place	Summary of Events and Information	Remarks and references to Appendices
MERRIS JAN 22ND	Route march 8 miles. Capt Campbell + 1 hon. reported. [illegible]. Heavy snow + hard during the day.	—
MERRIS JAN 23RD	Route March 9 miles. Raining No [illegible] hospital sick.	—
" JAN 24TH	Heavy thaw all day.	
	Battalion attended Church parade in the morning 1 officer + 1 N.C.O. attended at No 3 Field Squadron R.E. for instruction in wiring + throwing bombs + hand grenades. Capt and party of officers commanding Coy during afternoon for purpose of returning trenches. Adjutant attended conference at B.H.Q. at 2 p.m. Various M.O.'s were discussed mainly in connection with drawing + indenting for items such as Rifles for Rifles, Brazziers, Gloves, Iron Rods etc. Also a few points + questions + clothing. A damp raw day. Transport horses apparently feeling the effects of the weather on the air as 23 sick + cay, mostly several r pneumonia. All have now gone a little up in addition to the blanket. The question of Boots will be a very serious problem as the boots most in England type Forbidding are of a very much quality + are already failing to pieces. Every effort is being made to repair them but the shoemakers tag is at present unable key + worn axels in repairing books such as leather have now been ordered for all boots suffering from any severe evils but in the whole are getting better. 33 only attending sick tray against 77 yesterday. At all ranks paraded at 12.45. to go on the transfer of the 3Y division to extern information + up so to the Battalion exchanged letter No. numerals in the trenches tonight. Weapons + relief at the Battalion. Key battle being saying. Scene today from direction of Douches.	43

Army Form C. 2118.

WAR DIARY
INTELLIGENCE SUMMARY
(Erase heading not required.)

Instructions regarding War Diaries and Intelligence Summaries are contained in F.S. Regs., Part II. and the Staff Manual respectively. Title pages will be prepared in manuscript.

Hour, Date, Place	Summary of Events and Information	Remarks and references to Appendices
MERRIS JAN 25TH	The Battalion carried out a route march of 9 miles during the morning. Companies at disposal of Coy Commanders during the afternoon. Fat lecture returned from evening. The Trenches of the 2yd Division. A cold, damp, raw day. Very little firing heard during the day. A Companies team. Orders received at midnight for the number of Pack Regt. required immediately, when invaded in 500 packs, 84 enemy Bde list in readiness to move at a hour's notice from 9 am tomorrow until 9 am Saturday. One days provisions 2 Jan's in Supply Wagons of Train Transport ordered to be taken off Wagons and sent on Tuesday 26th Jan. Run of Ravel Farm Reserve.	See Appendix No 3 ₺ Notes of recent actions Appendix No 4
MERRIS JAN 26TH	Battalion carried out a route march of 9 miles during the morning. Companies at disposal of Coy. Coys during the afternoon. Captain F.N. Sumner proceeded at 1 P.M. to the Trenches of the 2yd Division to hold the right & gain information etc. Major T.A. White M.O. proceeded to visit the 2nd Batt. Suffolk Regt who are in Reserve at LA CRYPTE. Lt.Col. H. Ruggles Brise returned at 4 P.M. Command'y 2nd Suffolk Regt + Lieut Williams acting Aq 2nd Suffolk Regt. arrived at 1 P.M. Lieuts Hosmer we Well returned at 4 P.M. Battalion moved 4 hole croft in readiness to move at a moment's notice from 12 midnight tonight. This readiness fumes quickly returned to be in a reason of it hang the Kaiser Prussia in the 2/yE + the Germans night attempt it under Prussian's escurely. News re fighting along the line received.	Note Re News Appendix No 5
MERRIS JAN 27TH	Companies carried rifting. The Kaiser's Birthday, a quiet day of firing heard in the early morning. Our allied Corps for no attack —	₺

1247 W 3299 200,000 (E) 8/14 J.B.C. & A. Forms/C. 2118/11.

WAR DIARY
INTELLIGENCE SUMMARY

(Erase heading not required.)

Army Form C. 2118.

Instructions regarding War Diaries and Intelligence Summaries are contained in F. S. Regs., Part II. and the Staff Manual respectively. Title pages will be prepared in manuscript.

Hour, Date, Place	Summary of Events and Information	Remarks and references to Appendices
MERRIS JAN 28th	Field Marshal Sir John French inspected the 28 Division the 84th Bgt Brigade under Brigadier General Wanless O'Gowan was drawn up in a field near STRAZEELE. The inspection did not take long. Sir John French was received with a General Salute & then after walking down the front of each Battalion, Battalions moved up to Brig[?]. A number of bags of the 2nd Battalion can see her in coming from days Trenches & C.O.'s & S. Lieuts. Orders received to form two Platoons for working land grenades an Extra platoon to be called "The Grenadier Platoon" to be attached to the Right Company of the Battalion. Lieut. A.L. Wood & C=B. Bult selected to command the two Platoons.	B
MERRIS JAN 29th	Battalion practice digging of trenches in fields near billets. At night "Relief" of trenches was practiced, practiced[?]. Then got too lumbered up just before entering Trench, when a click seems to have been must last, only we have been the carried & on back. Otherwise quite a made. Recruit lads minutes trenches mist. Must an hag[?] done never up.	F

WAR DIARY
or
INTELLIGENCE SUMMARY.
(Erase heading not required.)

Army Form C. 2118.

Instructions regarding War Diaries and Intelligence Summaries are contained in F. S. Regs. Part II. and the Staff Manual respectively. Title pages will be prepared in manuscript.

Place	Date	Hour	Summary of Events and Information	Remarks and references to Appendices
MORRIS.	JAN 30th		Battalion Route March in morning. All Officers Men & Men of Battalion inoculated this just & outfits in whole oil, in preparation in orders going into the Trenches. Practised Night digging in evening after dark.	
MORRIS	JAN 31st		Very Cold, snow fell and still snowing. Church Parade cancelled. Battalion fitted in Trenches dug during previous day. Raining.	

A P P E N D I X   1.

BM 375

Appendix No 1

15th Jan., 1915.

84th Infantry Brigade

Order for March and Embarkation, 16th January.

(Refce. to 28th Div. Orders)

———————

1. The Brigade Starting Point, except for 1st Welch Regt., will be junction of HIGH STREET and SOUTHGATE STREET.

2. Battalions will pass this point as under :-

   2nd North'd Fus.   8.45 a.m. approaching via UPPER HIGH STREET
   2nd Ches. R.   8.55 a.m.   "   "   "   "   "
   1st Suff. R.   9.5 a.m.   "   "   JEWRY STREET.

3. 1st Welch R. will join the column via BEAUFORT ROAD at 9.22 a.m., in rear of 1st Suff. R.

4. Train wagons with Battalions (6) will follow each 1st line transport.

5. The march is considered as beginning at 9.10 a.m. (Div. Starting Point): no ten minutes halt will be made at 8.50 a.m.

   Brigade Head Quarters under the Brigade Machine Gun Officer will join the main column via BEAUFORT ROAD at 10.30 a.m.

   Watches will be checked by representatives for orders at 6.0 p.m. to-day.

at 1.0 p.m.
each Battalion
M.G.Officer

H Walford
Captain
Brigade Major
84th Infty. Bde.

BM 383   To 1st Suff R.

With reference to the March Table for to-morrow issued with the Divisional Orders to-day, the hour of passing the Chandlers Ford point will be advanced by five minutes.

2nd Northd Fus. will therefore pass this point at 10.55 a.m.,   2nd Ches. R. at 11.5 a.m.

1st Suff. R. at 11.25 a.m. ? 11-15

1st Welch R. at 12.33 p.m. ? 11-25

The times for the Southampton Common point, and arrival at No 2 Dock Gates remain the same as on ~~the same as on~~ the March Table.

15/1/15 7.40 pm

Walford
Captain
Brigade Major
84th Infantry Bde.

Recd 8.15 pm

BM 376

To

2nd. North'd. Fus.
1st Suff. R.
2nd. Ches. R.
1st Welch R.

Under instructions received from A.A.& Q.M.G. units embarking to-morrow will start fifteen minutes before the time given in March Table, but they will arrive at the Docks at the time given in the Table.

~~Acknowledge receipt~~

The times given in the Brigade Order (BM 376) will all be advanced fifteen minutes.

Acknowledge receipt.

E.H.Walford

Captain
Brigade Major
84th Infty. Bde.

15/1/15.   2.35 p.m.

S E C R E T.

Distribution List of Embarkation Orders for January, 16.

    1 to each Unit embarking.
    1 to G.O.C.
    1 to G.S.O. 1.
    1 to General Staff
    1 to "A"
    1 to G.O.C. Royal Artillery.
    1 to Embarkation Southampton.
    1 to Remounts.

SECRET.

28TH DIVISION ORDERS FOR EMBARKATION.
15th January, 1915.

1. Troops shown on the accompanying tables will march to Southampton for the purpose of embarkation in accordance with the March Table.

2. The times given in the March Table must be strictly adhered to, and units must preserve strict march discipline otherwise they will be unable to enter the Docks at the required time.

3. All vehicles will be marked on the near side with the serial number (see March Table)

4. Any man or vehicle falling out will be instructed to report to the Officer at No.2 gate, and will be given a written order with the number of the berth and the name of the ship on it.

5. On arriving at the Dock Gate the Officer Commanding the unit will load his unit, and an officer will be detailed to bring up the rear of each unit throughout the march. This officer will report to the officer at the gate if any part of his Unit has fallen out.

6. Civilian guides will be provided at the Dock Gates to lead Units to their berths.

7. Units with vehicles will close up to the far end of the berth shed so as not to block the road and to economise space.

8. The entrance to the berth shed will be kept clear in order not to block other troops who may have to enter.

9. Nobody except those actually on duty will be allowed in the docks.

10. Unfit horses which are not going to accompany units will be returned to Mr. Tatts, Stanmore Lane, or to the Remount Depot, Southgate Street, Winchester, by 2.0pm on the day before that on which Units concerned are detailed to march to Southampton

11. All horses showing distress on the march will be changed, and all deficiencies of horses in Units will be made up by the Remount Department at the Cross Roads at STONEHAM (1 mile N. of cross roads at N.E.corner of SOUTHAMPTON COMMON), or at the railway bridge at SWAYTHLING, according as Units are ordered to march via CHANDLER'S FORD or EASTLEIGH.

12. Horses will be watered in the Docks and fed after Embarkation.

13. Acknowledge.

Loch.
Lieut.Colonel,
General Staff, 28th Division.

SECRET.

MARCH and EMBARKATION TABLE for SATURDAY, 16th JANUARY.

Reference :—WINCHESTER MAP, 1 inch to 1 mile.

Serial Number	UNIT	Time of March	Starting Point	ROUTE	Hour of passing Railway at CHANDLER'S FORD, immediately N. of Bridge over Road Junction	Hours of passing Cross Roads at N.E. end of SOUTHAMPTON COMMON	Hour of Arrival at No. 2 Dock Gate	SHIP	Berth
17	Squadron Surrey Yeomanry	9 a.m.	Road Junction at PITT	HURSLEY — CHANDLER'S FORD—SOUTHAMPTON COMMON—Left branch of AVENUE—ST. MARY'S ROAD—ST. MARY'S STREET—THREEFIELD LANE—LATIMER STREET	10.50 a.m.	12 noon	1. 0 p.m.	KINGSTONIAN	46
18	2nd Northumberland Fusiliers	9.10 a.m.	Road Junction 1 mile North of COMPTON	OTTERBOURNE—CHANDLER'S FORD—SOUTHAMPTON COMMON—Left branch of AVENUE—ST. MARY'S ROAD—ST. MARY'S STREET—THREEFIELD LANE—LATIMER STREET	11. 0 a.m.	12.10 p.m.	1.10 p.m.	AUSTRALIND	25
19	2nd Cheshires	9.20 a.m.	,,	,,	11.10 a.m.	12.20 p.m.	1.20 p.m.	CITY OF CHESTER	33
20	1st Suffolks	9.30 a.m.	,,	,,	11.20 a.m.	12.30 p.m.	1.30 p.m.	MOUNT TEMPLE	38
21	1st Welsh	9.40 a.m.	,,	,,	11.30 a.m.	12.40 p.m.	1.40 p.m.	CARDIGANSHIRE	44
22	Headquarters 31st Brigade R.F.A. and 69th Battery R.F.A.	11. 0 a.m.	Road Junction at S. Corner of Park of BRAMBRIDGE HOUSE (2 miles South of TWYFORD CHURCH)	AILBROOK—EASTLEIGH—SWAYTHLING—BURGESS STREET—SOUTHAMPTON COMMON—Left branch of AVENUE—ST. MARY'S ROAD—ST. MARY'S STREET—THREEFIELD LANE—LATIMER STREET	...	12.50 p.m.	1.50 p.m.	KINGSTONIAN	46
23	100th Battery R.F.A.	10. 0 a.m.	As for 2nd Northumberland Fusiliers	via TWYFORD, then follow H.Q. 31st Bde. R.F.A.	...	1. 0 p.m.	2. 0 p.m.	AUSTRALIND	25
24	No. 3 Section Div. Signal Company	10.10 a.m.	As for 2nd Northumberland Fusiliers	As for 2nd Northumberland Fusiliers	12 noon	1.10 p.m.	2.10 p.m.	CITY OF CHESTER	33
25	103rd Battery R.F.A.	11.30 a.m.	As for H.Q. 31st Brigade R.F.A.	As for H.Q. 31st Brigade R.F.A.	12.20 p.m.	1.20 p.m.	2.20 p.m.	MOUNT TEMPLE	38
26*	3rd London Field Ambulance	10.30 a.m.	As for 2nd Northumberland Fusiliers	As for 2nd Northumberland Fusiliers	12.30 p.m.	1.30 p.m.	2.30 p.m.	KINGSTONIAN	46
	3rd London Field Ambulance (Vehicles)	,,	,,	,,	,,	,,	,,	AUSTRALIND	25
27	3rd Brigade Company Div. Train	10.40 a.m.	,,	,,	,,	1.40 p.m.	2.40 p.m.	CITY OF CHESTER	33
28	84th Infantry Brigade Headquarters	10.50 a.m.	,,	,,	12.40 p.m.	1.50 p.m.	2.50 p.m.	MOUNT TEMPLE	38
29	31st Brigade Ammunition Column	12.10 p.m.	As for H.Q. 31st Brigade R.F.A.	As for H.Q. 31st Brigade, R.F.A.	...	2. 0 p.m.	3. 0 p.m.	KINGSTONIAN	46

NOTE 26*.—Drivers and horses will leave vehicles at Berth 25, proceed to Berth 46, and embark on the "KINGSTONIAN."

WARREN & SON, LTD, WINCHESTER.

NOT APPENDIX

APPENDIX 2.

A COPY ISSUED TO EACH O. C. UNIT.

APPENDIX No 2

To..
    Military Embarkation Officer,
        SOUTHAMPTON.

    Herewith attached copy of a paper concerning entraining routine at HAVRE.

    Could you please have it handed to the Commanding Officer of the 1st. Infantry Battn. of the 28th. Division to embark at Southampton Docks ?

               (sd)   E. GROGAN, MAJOR.
HAVRE,   G. S. 28th. DIVISION.
  13. 1. '15.

To..
    Officer Commanding 1st. Infantry Battn.
       of 28th. Division to embark at Southampton.

    Herewith paper (A) on routine at HAVRE.   Will you please cause it to be passed to Commanders of Battalions, which follow you and embark on the same day, after you have perused it.

               (sd)   E. GROGAN, MAJOR.
HAVRE,   G. S. 28th. DIVISION.
  13. 1. '15.

"A"

THE FOLLOWING POINTS REGARDING THE ENTRAINING
ROUTINE AT HAVRE MAY BE OF USE TO O. C. UNITS

(1) An advance party will probably be required to take over the train, the same party should be employed to hand it over at the destination.

(2) Carriages are told off and men are marched straight into them.   Kits and Rifles put away and men then fall in for fatigues.

(2)

(3) Following fatigue parties will be required:-

    (a) Two of 50 men each under an Officer to load wagons.
    (b) One of 40 men under representative of Quarter-Master Department to draw rations and forage.
    (c) One of 20 men to draw and distribute sand in Horse Trucks.
    (d) One of 30 men to assist in entraining horses.

(4) A Picket of 50 men to guard approaches to Train will be required.

(5) If no benches exist in trucks for men, hay will be drawn by Quarter-Masters.

(6) Eight Horses to a truck. Large and small horses should be mixed. It is impossible to put 8 large horses in one truck. Horses are tied up to rings above. Breast ropes in front. The latter to be provided by Units.

(7) On arrival at Station horses will be formed up where shown, harness removed but head collars kept on.

(8) Sand must be put in each truck. Nosebags put on and buckets kept out.

(9) Two men to be told off to travel in each horse truck. If possible, non-smokers, as no smoking allowed. One truss of hay and two sacks of oats to be put in each truck. Harness in the centre of the Gangway.

(10) If horses are refractory when loading, build wings to ramps with trusses of hay.

(11) An Officer should be told off to assist the Regimental Transport Officer in entraining the horses.

                              (sd) E. GROGAN, MAJOR.
                                    G. S. 28th. DIVISION.

HAVRE,
   13. 1. '15.

APPENDIX 3.

Notes on Trenches   Appendix No 3
March to trenches in great coats   8
Horses left with transport where ordered
   by brigade
2 Co's in firing line & support 2 in reserve
Take up all tools with them
During relief whole Co goes up in file, then
   take up platoons or trench full at a time.
Relieve firing line daily
Teas & rations come up with Q^r M^r daily
about 5
  Reserve Co's have tea & get their rations then
1 Co at a time relieve firing line & support.
Firing line cook bacon & tea over brazier
Co's should each have a Primus.
All digging done at night
See parapet is thick
Repair trench
Get communication trench into order.
Reg^t has 70000 rounds.
Men 120 each. 16 boxes per Co^y in firing line
MG's take up all their belt boxes
Brushwood with planks on good for trenches
2 Stretcher bearers with morphia tablets per Coy
   in firing line.
Wounded removed in dark
M.O. at H^d Q^rs perhaps dressing station further back.
Dig latrines inconspicuous ones behind fire trenches
Use tins during day time.
1 Very pistol for each Coy to give light.

Draw pails for baking out coke & charcoal
also braziers, these can be improvised with
biscuit tins.
Get gum boots for men
Don't show sandbags on parapet cover with earth.
Reserves can make hurdles for roads, fascines.
Men can cook bacon & make tea on braziers
Braziers must not smoke or show a light.
Men in support & reserve trenches must not show
Transport Officer & Qr Mr stay with transport.
Only telephones used
Get rid of bulk of helios & lamps
Replace with shovels
1 Pick to 3 shovels at present
About 6 telephones wanted
MG Officer stays in firing line; if you can relieve
   men do.
MGs down in daytime, up at night.
Glycerine required for MGs.

APPENDIX 4.

APPENDIX No 4

Admiralty issued the following announcement early this morning:-
"British Patrolling Squadron of Battle Cruisers, and light Cruisers under Vice Admiral Sir D. Beatty, with a Destroyer Flotilla under Commodore Tyrwhitt, sighted four German Battle Cruisers, several light Cruisers, and a number of Destroyers making for the English Coast. The enemy at once made for home at high speed. They were pursued, and 9.30 a.m. action was joined between British "Lion", "Tiger", "Princess Royal", "New Zealand", and "Indomitable", the German "Derfflinger", "Seydlitz", "Moltke" and "Blucher".

Soon after 1 o'clock "Blucher" capsized and sank; two other Battle Cruisers seriously damaged, but escaped. No British ships lost, and casualties slight. One hundred and twenty three survivors rescued from "Blucher's" Crew of 885.

Sixteen aeroplanes sunk by Russian Fleet in Black Sea, destined for use of Army in Caucasus.

On January 6th last, the "Australia", the Flagship of the Commonwealth Navy captured and sunk a German liner which was acting as a supply ship for German Cruisers. Officers and crew taken prisoners

----

APPENDIX 5.

APPENDIX No 5.

news communicated by 28th Division is published

ation :-

re ... y the ight of our First Army and the left of the French were heavily attacked. Our front to East of CUINCHY at first pierced, as well as outer Trench due East of GIVENCHY. Germans also broke into GIVENCHY village; five attacks from N.E. of village repulsed. Counter attack delivered and Trenches regained except just South of the Canal, where line has been slightly re-adjusted. All attacks on French repulsed. First Corps report taking two officers and fifty men one other ranks prisoners. Enemy lost heavily, about three German officers and three hundred other ranks killed on main BETHUNE - LE BASSEE road by machine gun fire. BETHUNE shelled intermittently during day.

APPENDIX 6.

SK 164 Eighty fourth Bde APPENDIX No. 6

The following report has been obtained from Capt Walker commd'g new P trenches

Manned by Germans   P trench
                                         ┌─────── wire ───────┐
R trench invisible but   │   │
talking was heard from it   │   200 yds   │
                              Z   │   open ground   │
                            50yds   │   │
German redoubt   ┌────────────┤   │
with 2 MGs   │ P₁ P₂ ──┤   │
                            │ a a a a a │   │
                            │ new P's   │   │
                            │ thin copse│
                            ditch

P₁ & P₂ were the trenches we took over. they were about 10 yds apart. The Germans had a redoubt at Z with 2 MGs which were higher than our trench and commanded it. Z is strongly built of sandbags and makes it P₁ P₂ hard to hold. The right ends of P₁ P₂ are deep in water owing to the slope in the ground. The 6%'s tried to start a drain but were unable to. There was a lot of wire entanglement of knife rest pattern

on N side of P trench. Many of the men in P₁ P₂ had to sit up to their waists in water to avoid MG fire from Z. Capt Walker was unable to join up P₁ P₂ although he tried to. He only found about 6 shovels in the trench.

When we took over from the Middlesex there were about 4 men in P₁, and about a dozen in P₂ but there were quite 50 in the wood in rear lying down.

He found 1 wounded man in P₁ and 2 wounded men & 1 wounded officer left by the Middx in P₂ we sent these back during the night we took over.

They also left a MG in the mud & water at the bottom of the trench. I regret we were unable to bring this away; its bipod had been hit several times.

18-2-15
                    W.B. Wallace Lt Col
                    Commd'g 1/Suffolk Regt

Sk
145. 84th Bde

Lieut Harrison who I sent to take
command of N trench on Capt Wood
Martin being killed reports as follows

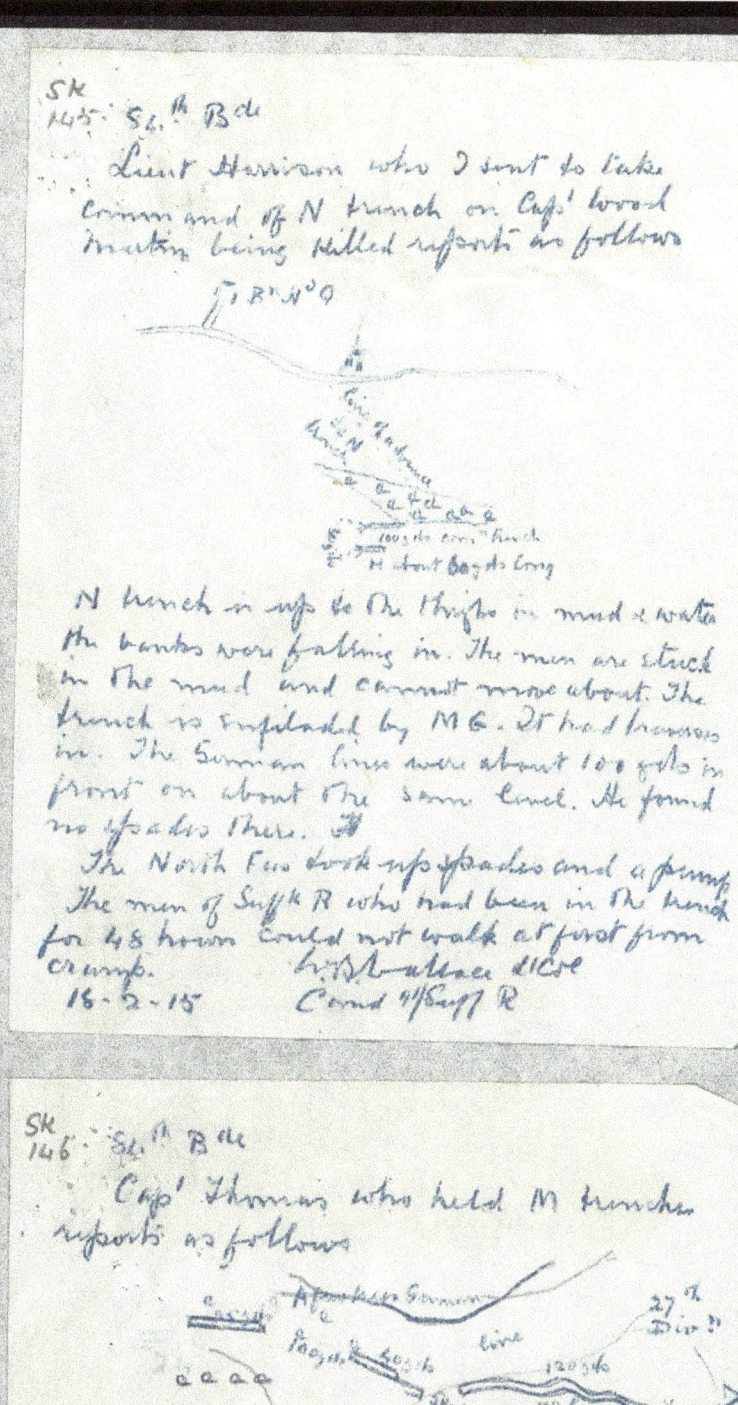

N trench is up to the thighs in mud & water
the banks were falling in. The men are stuck
in the mud and cannot move about. The
trench is enfiladed by M.G. It had traverses
in. The German lines were about 100 yds in
front on about the same level. He found
no spades there.

The North Fus took up spades and a pump
The men of Suff R who had been in the trench
for 48 hours could not walk at first from
cramp.   W.S. Wallace ½ Col
18-2-15   Comd 4/Suff R

Sk
146. 84th Bde

Capt Thomas who held M trenches
reports as follows

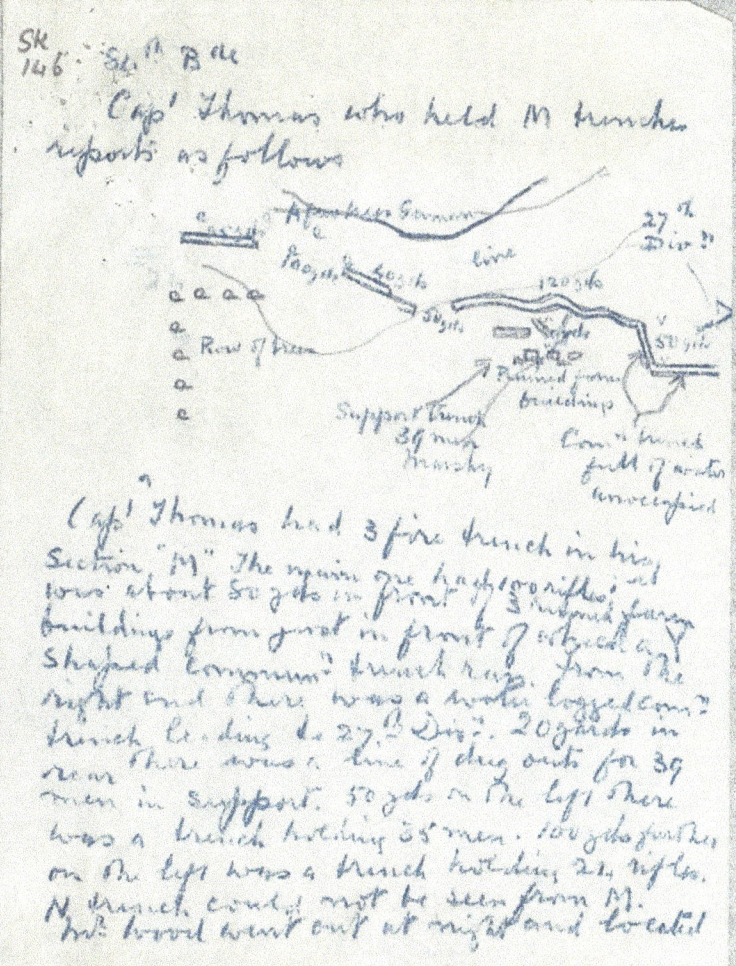

Capt Thomas had 3 fire trench in his
Section "M". The main one had 100 rifles, it
was about 50 yds in front of 3 ruined farm
buildings from just in front of which a
shaped communn trench ran from the
right and there was a waterlogged commn
trench leading to 27th Divn. 20 yds in
rear there was a line of dug outs for 39
men in support. 50 yds on the left there
was a trench holding 35 men. 100 yds further
on the left was a trench holding 24 rifles.
N trench could not be seen from M.
Mr Wood went out at night and located

N. trench 200 or 300 yds to their up, front.

The German lines were about 200 yds away, the main trench could only see the German line where it came over the crest.

The 2 smaller trenches could see more of the German lines.

A number of sandbags were found in the trench and were used with the ones brought by the Coy to improve the parapet.

Some boards were found near the parapet of the main trench which were used to form a small berm to stand on, this kept the men out of the wet.

In the other 2 trenches baling had to be used but they were still very wet.

The parapets were bullet proof.

W. K. Wallace 2Lt
Comdt 1/Suffolk Regt

16-2-15

APPENDIX 7.

'84 C Batt.   APPENDIX No 7

The following is the report on the events which led to the greater part of "C" Coy being missing.

The Battn relieved the 3rd Battn Middlesex Regt in the trenches on the night of 15th–16th Feby.

On arriving at Hd Qrs of the Battn the Company guides proceeded to relieve the trenches.

It had been reported to me that O trench had previously been captured by the enemy but had been retaken by the Buffs that evening.

"C" Coy under Capt Jourdain, led by 2 guides of the 3rd Middlesex Regt was ordered to relieve this trench.

About 4 a.m. 16th Feby Sgt Allen C Coy came to Bn Hd Qrs and reported verbally that Capt Jourdain had got into O trench and found that only ½ had been captured, that there was a big traverse across the trench

and that the Germans were on the other side. Capt Jourdain's portion of the trench was crowded and he was using his grenades and wanted more, and that the enemy had two machine guns in the trench. He was proceeding to investigate and would report again shortly and see if he could charge the enemy and drive them out.

Lt [?] E Surrey Regt who had been in the attack which partially recaptured O trench came to Bn Hd Qrs and said that he had seen a Maxim with several men lying round it on his way from O trench. He said that after he left O trench the enemy opened a very heavy Maxim fire all over the ground in rear of O trench.

Sgt Allen was sent back to get into touch with C Coy, but he was shot. He carried a message to Capt Jourdain to hold O trench and that

reinforcement would be sent.
On the 2 platoons which were in
reserve on the Canal bank coming
up to HQ No 4 it was becoming
quite light and I decided that
it was too light for such a small
party to make a bayonet attack
in face of the heavy fire the enemy
were bringing to bear.

I received a message from N
trench that O trench had been
captured at dawn

Lt S Wallace 2/Coy
Comd 4/Suffolk Regt

22-2-15

84th Bde.

28th Div.

Battalion went with Bde
to 5th Div. 22.2.15.
....

WAR DIARY.

1st SUFFOLK REGIMENT.

FEBRUARY.

1 9 1 5.

......

WAR DIARY
of
INTELLIGENCE SUMMARY.
(Erase heading not required.)

Army Form C. 2118.

Place	Date	Hour	Summary of Events and Information	Remarks and references to Appendices
MERRIS	FEB 1st		1st Line Transport & Train Transport left MERRIS at 7.15 p.m. & proceeded by road route under 2nd Lieut Goodhall & Lt. Leut. Ray Elliott to	(Sgd)
MERRIS	FEB 2nd		VLAMERTINGHE. Left BILLETS at 11.50 a.m. arrived at Bus Column at 12.30 p.m. Started embussing at 12.40 p.m. Battalion entrained at 1.15 p.m. 38 Buses allotted 24 officers 893 other ranks. If the right number of Buses had been present to time the embussing would have been completed in 15 mins easily, as each bus had was filled off before leaving BILLETS. Bus convoy left at 2 p.m. arrived VLAMERTINGHE at 6 p.m. debussed & marched to bivouac about 1½ miles. Left Bivouac 9 p.m. & arrived at YPRES by road under cover of dark & went into Infantry Barracks Rue at 11 p.m.	(Sgd)
YPRES	FEB 3rd		C & D Coys started at 9.30 a.m. to take supplies and to Transport Coy arrived back at 6 a.m. 1st Line & Train Transport returned to VLAMERTINGHE at 6.30 a.m. except the pack Cobs, Ammn Wagn & Limbers gun wagon & Water Carts, which remained at Infantry Bks. YPRES.	(Sgd)

WAR DIARY
INTELLIGENCE SUMMARY

Army Form C. 2118.

Instructions regarding War Diaries and Intelligence Summaries are contained in F.S. Regs., Part II. and the Staff Manual respectively. Title pages will be prepared in manuscript.

(Erase heading not required.)

Hour, Date, Place	Summary of Events and Information	Remarks and references to Appendices
YPRES FEB 3rd	Night of 3/4 Feb. Battalion standing by to move at a moments notice. 5.0 am Bomb sent to trenches with extra ammunition.	
YPRES FEB 4th	C + D Coys under Capt Cooper ordered to BLAUWPOORT FARM at 7 P.M. on 4th to report to 83rd Inf Bde. were relieved this afternoon to 2nd Line. A + B Coys returned by the same at 8.30 P.M. Men had been sent away during relief to 1st Welch Regt in Trenches. [B Coy relieved at 9 p.m. having left ammunition one at BDE H.Q. Capt Misson having gone on to BLAUWPOORT met Return for 1 Welsh Regt. Capt Wood Martin ordered at 5.30 p.m. Capt Wilson + party arrived back at 9.40 p.m.] C + D Coys arrived at Bde H.Q. at 5.30 p.m.	
BLAUWEPOORT FARM FEB 5th	Headquarters of Battn with A + B Coys arrived at 12.20 am from YPRES. At 12.40 a.m. reported to Bde H.Q. our arrival. C + D Coys under Capt Cooper ordered off at 1 AM to occupy 2nd line of defence + to go front with the EAST YORKS + K.O.Y.L.I. At 1.15 AM Headquarters returned to Batt H.Q. at Blauwpoort Farm + reported to Hd Qrs. At 5 am YPRES + K.O.Y.L.I. in a wood. Capt Boger with D + Coys arrived at the support Trenches ordered were occupied by about 40 men of E YORKS under Command of a Major. 2 coys of E YORKS were in the firing line. Had these been relieved + were at ROUGENT HALL. Capt Cooper took over Trenches until No Man of E YORKS arrived well.	

WAR DIARY
INTELLIGENCE SUMMARY
(Erase heading not required.)

Army Form C. 2118.

Hour, Date, Place	Summary of Events and Information	Remarks and references to Appendices
VERBRANDEN MOLEN FARM 1/11/17		
2 AM	Arrived at headquarters 2nd Yorks regt. Relief of 2nd Yorks regt in the trenches completed at 6.12 AM, a further 2½ Coy B & C/11/5 and B Coy Telephone communication with 15 Coy on N of Railway already laid, also on with H.Q. Bde. Communication with D Coy on Right obtained by means of Runner Regtl Telephone.	
8 AM	Telephonic communication with Bde Sup Regt + 73 Coy broken down.	B
10.45 AM	" " " " repaired	
11 AM	Everything quiet, sent into Bde H.Q. at 10.30 A.M. a report for rum, sand bags, cake, + 40,000 rounds ammunition. Casualties to date: Officers killed + 2 wounded.	
1 PM	Batt. Headquarters heavily shelled, no damage done, but two shells (high explosive) came very close to house + stood up a good deal, dirt etc. All were led to long before this there is trouble is knocked down I a tree + too we here are to be killed or wounded etc. a shot dangerous position as German have been to have got our the 20yr fairly accurately—	
4.45 PM	Received message from Capt Cooper D Coy right of line, that B Coy F. YORKS on his right had retired into his trench + he had heard that F. YORKS had orders retirement + that he, Capt Cooper, was going also as per what caused the same.	
4.50 PM	Capt Cooper reported "YORKS" have retired into our right trench.	C

WAR DIARY / INTELLIGENCE SUMMARY

Army Form C. 2118.

Instructions regarding War Diaries and Intelligence Summaries are contained in F.S. Regs., Part II. and the Staff Manual respectively. Title pages will be prepared in manuscript.

Hour, Date, Place	Summary of Events and Information	Remarks and references to Appendices
FEB 5th	am Losing on, attack by Germans on my right flank. His information sent to H.Q 84" INF Bde & also to 2 Batt 3rd Cheshire Regt at BLAUWEPOORT FARM. & Headquarters were asked to send the 2 Batt Cheshire Regt to reinforce our Right flank. Instructions were sent to both to try on German line, but that if the Batt. should be forced to retire, the reserve trench to be taken up.	
6pm	Report received from Capt for Ammunition & Ammunition. to Bde H.Q. 2 Coys 2 Cheshire Regt from BLAUWEPOORT FARM dispatched Batt H.Q. at 6.50 pm on way to support D Coy.	B
6.45pm	Further demands for Ammunition sent in	
6.45pm	Message received from D Coy that they were looking on alright & no German advance could be seen on the right.	
7pm	D Coy & Cyclists Platoon sent to last known task a below Zero & one platoon to trench running at right angles to the right. K.O.Y.L.I. who had never relieved 2F YORKS are to hurry up their reserve tonight & newly relieved of Kent trench. K.O.Y.L.I. relief that YORK & LANCS on this night can retire, this trench been done to by K.O.Y.L.I.	B
7.50pm	Further urgent demands from Capt for Ammunition. Ox D Coy again told K.O.Y.L.I. return to trenches that had evacuated.	
8.40pm	Message received that Ammunition was coming from YPRES. Attend Capt to send Guides to Bde H.Q. to guide Carrying parties to trenches.	B

WAR DIARY or INTELLIGENCE SUMMARY

Army Form C. 2118.

Hour, Date, Place	Summary of Events and Information	Remarks and references to Appendices
FEB 5th 9 p.m.	Ammunition arrived at Bn H.Q. Sent 16 boxes at once to D Coy & Capt. Lee remainder to C & B Coys.	
11 p.m.	Returns arrived by fatigue party of 2nd Cheshire Regt. handed to Capt Ingram from Bn to our left. Cheshire men who had been assisting in holding the line before, were absolutely dead beat, owing to H.E shells in trenches the day before, and the heat of taking return ammunition etc. to trenches was very great, so that many items were dumped in communication trenches & left to be collected afterwards by our own the following one.	
FEB 6th 12.40 a.m.	Sent to D Coy asking if attack of N.O. 4 L.I had taken place & that Bn H.Q. over by Bn of 2nd Cheshire Regt to return to BLAUWEPOORT FARM Hunter's Battalion nearing Hdr situation.	[B]
3 a.m.	D Coy wired that all is quiet on Right & that Cheshires are to return to BLAUWEPOORT FARM if situation warrants it.	
2.10 p.m.	C Coy report all quiet [Blair-Biggs stopt gage by butler or slush, nothing heard until 2.15 well at duty.] D Coy report all quiet.	
y a.s p.m		
10.30 p.m	Bn Genuine Western 84 Infantry arrived at Bn H.Q.	
11 p.m.	First Coy of 2nd Cheshire Regt. dawned Bn H.Q. in relief of our Coys in trenches.	
11.30 p.	Bn & gone speasiful to quiet trenches with C.O.	
FEB 7th 4.15 a.m.	Relief completed. He & 2nd Coys. left with D Coy Hd. 2nd D & B Coys proceeded to Rd Gds YPRES BLAUWEPOORT FARM. A.V.E. + M.B.s	[B]

WAR DIARY
INTELLIGENCE SUMMARY.
(Erase heading not required.)

Army Form C. 2118.

Instructions regarding War Diaries and Intelligence Summaries are contained in F.S. Regs., Part II. and the Staff Manual respectively. Title pages will be prepared in manuscript.

Hour, Date, Place		Summary of Events and Information	Remarks and references to Appendices
YPRES	FEB 4th 7 AM	Batt Head Qrs. D & B Coys arrived Infantry Bks YPRES. Men very tired owing to continued fatigue in addition to fighting in the trenches. Barracks very dirty & very crowded. Immediate need is now to clean them & get some attention turned to an outbreak of Scabies. Ypres Stat'y Barracks unduly & Staff Infy Tar 84 L.F.Bde.	
"	8 "	½ Batt'n remained at YPRES all day. No letters except a good wash. (not in Bed?).	B
"	9 "	Remained at YPRES preparing to proceed again to trenches in evening to relieve the 2nd Border Regt.	B
"	8 pm	Batt H.Q. D & B Coys left YPRES to relieve 2nd Border Regt in trenches in approx. section west at YPRES–Commines Railway, S/ma, & Returns	
"		½ Coy taken by Major S. to BLAUWEPOORT FARM.	
"	7.30 PM	Arrived BLAUWEPOORT FARM. Having gone again a short cut across country to avoid the open roads at TROIS ROIS which is very ½ heavily shelled. Although the route was carefully reconnoitred before hand by day & the Free Rd was very slow, it took ½ hour Lieut. B Coy which was in rear that took & it took 1¾ hours to again trench, which shows the near necessity of the extreme caution required to maintain touch in a long column as night.	
"	10.15 PM	Coys proceeded from BLAUWEPOORT FARM. & take over own section	B
"	9th 3 AM	of trenches on relief. Relief completed. Reported to Bde Head Quarters.	

(73989) W4141—463. 400,000. 9/14. H.&J.Ltd. Forms/C. 2118/10.

WAR DIARY
INTELLIGENCE SUMMARY.
(Erase heading not required.)

Army Form C. 2118.

Instructions regarding War Diaries and Intelligence Summaries are contained in F.S. Regs., Part II. and the Staff Manual respectively. Title pages will be prepared in manuscript.

Hour, Date, Place	Summary of Events and Information	Remarks and references to Appendices
VERDRANDEN MOLEN FFR Q1S		
FEB 6th 7:50 AM	C Coy had 3 men wounded owing to BLAUWPOORT FARM on cleaning it, starting what practice without loss. Trench or RYPATS won line (D Coy) went very bad. Has remained once lost by the Supps but retaken about 3 am by Lt-Royal of Fusiliers. This trench almost untenable owing to deep 2ft. water running inwards — but being enfiladed by observation trench running towards the Ferry, who are apposite that away from parapet not Rearparapet. D Coy gave 50 yards of their trench to Fusiliers. Part of trench repaired by be Coy of Fusiliers (Major Baker) to 85th Regt. Bde. attempt non Telephone. "That the death of trench intolerable unless parapet dry & reserve of platoon are carried by improve & upper parapet	B
9 AM	No 7914 Pte Last D Coy killed	
9 AM	No 16164 Pte Rider & No 7961 Pte Meeck A Coy killed D Coy report that our artillery shelled German trenches in front of their line very severely during morning. First Regt killed Tender knot of railway spare to Bee HQ through our Bde HQ. That German kindly shelled their own trench, so shells falling into advanced trenches.	
1:30 PM	Capt Wood-Martin reported that a British shell fell into his trench & wounded his men. This shell accidentally fired from	B

WAR DIARY
INTELLIGENCE SUMMARY.
(Erase heading not required.)

Army Form C. 2118.

Hour, Date, Place	Summary of Events and Information	Remarks and references to Appendices
VERBRANDEN MOLEN F.15.q.5		
2 P.M.	2nd Lieut R.F.A. informed Bde. Hqrs. 31st Inf. Bde. Capt Wood Martin gave German had been shelling the top of his trenches by Railway bridge but had stopped. Asked him in particular as to direction of fire etc, but he could not tell. Cpl Wood Martin after German again shelling his left, sent him to gain as much information as possible as to direction & locality of German battery (?) (I moved this mor. our Artillery (Kemmel Bde Hqrs.)	
2:15 P.M.		
3:20 P.M.	Bastrain Keep quarters heavily shelled by German Artillery about 40 shells burst in vicinity of our Building and always between except one of our old memory. 20 casualties.	
	Preston officer went to D Coy's trenches at 1 P.M. to be a Company commander now, he however died upon M.O. put later. M.B. attended badly wounded man of Royal Fusiliers in our Trench on right, to have lost their Padre, was in an awful condition, & got up walls & got presently but were 110 wounded to B.A.R. Hqs at 3.20 P.m.	
8 P.M.	All wounded (including a number of Royal Fus.) who had been sent to Batt. Hqs left in Field Ambulances.	

Army Form C. 2118.

WAR DIARY
INTELLIGENCE SUMMARY.
(Erase heading not required.)

Instructions regarding War Diaries and Intelligence Summaries are contained in F.S. Regs., Part II. and the Staff Manual respectively. Title pages will be prepared in manuscript.

Hour, Date, Place	Summary of Events and Information	Remarks and references to Appendices
VERBRANDENMOLEN FEB 9th	All telephone communication with Coys (except D) + with Bde H.Q. broken down by heavy shell fire at 2:30 p.m.	
8 p.m.	all telephone lines repaired.	
1 p.m.	Return communication etc arrived at Batt. H.Q. & partys consisting of 2 Cheshire Regt & 1st Country Yeoman Regt. Bde Major reported that P.J. Lieut Manyford Steven was killed near Bde Headquarters whilst bringing rations up to Coys. Received order Bde Headquarters. R.O.Y. L1 appears came up to great trenches as they are going into storm. Bde being relieved by the 83rd in the night of the 11-12th inst.	B
FEB 10th		
8 a.m.	Coys report all quiet	
11 a.m.	All Coys manned to keep under cover as own Artillery are going to fire on German trenches in Square I 35 a 8.1 and I 35 C.Y.Y.	
3:30 p.m.	order received re relief tonight. Relief went to Coys. Batt H.Q. C + D Places to YPRES. B + N + M 45 to BEAUREPORT FARM.	
5 p.m.	Batt. Headquarters relieved. So steps no damage.	
7 FEB 10th 11 p.m. 12:30 a.m.	2 Cheshire Regt started to relieve us Relief completed.	B

Army Form C. 2118.

WAR DIARY
or
INTELLIGENCE SUMMARY.
(Erase heading not required.)

Instructions regarding War Diaries and Intelligence Summaries are contained in F.S. Regs., Part II and the Staff Manual respectively. Title pages will be prepared in manuscript.

Hour, Date, Place	Summary of Events and Information	Remarks and references to Appendices
YPRES FEB 10. 3 AM 11.	B⁰ Headquarters. C & D Coys answered infantry R.H.S. on Burning 12ᵗʰ County of London Regt Bedits on entering YPRES. Patrolsen was heard by Sentry, Sentry was very frightened & although no one noted fired into the middle of the mounted Pt ward Lynathin.	
2 P.M.	Dr Chamberlain D Coy tried by Field General Court Martial for sleeping whilst on Sentry in the Trenches.	£I

Army Form C. 2118.

WAR DIARY
or
INTELLIGENCE SUMMARY.
(Erase heading not required.)

Instructions regarding War Diaries and Intelligence Summaries are contained in F. S. Regs., Part II. and the Staff Manual respectively. Title pages will be prepared in manuscript.

Hour, Date, Place		Summary of Events and Information	Remarks and references to Appendices
YPRES FEB 11TH	5 P.M.	Head Quarters, C & A Companies + 1 Plat. Transport left YPRES to go into Billets near OUDERDOM for rest. B + C Coys + Machine Gunners in support at BLAUWEPOORT FARM ordered to leave YPRES at 6.30 P.M. & proceed straight to Billeting Area.	
	8.30 P.M.	H.Q. C. & A Coys arrived in Billeting Area + went into Billets	
Nº OUDERDOM FEB 12TH	2.30 A.M.	B & D Coys + Machine Gunners arrived Billeting Area. Went into Billets. Billets very scattered. Adjutant hadn't received them during night. Received news that Coys to proceed to HAZEBROUCK to entrain but hadn't orders sent to Coys assembly by party who that are to proceed.	
"	7 A.M.	Adjutant rode round Billets all correct. Sent orders to Bde Headquarters at RUSSEROOM.	
	2 P.M.	Orange Received from. Bn. INF. BDE H.Q. that 85th Inf Bde sent that 11th Bgt Corps is being attacked. What about? No lost sent + orders to move at a moment's notice. Coys warned. Orders being sent round at 2.5 P.M. to come look at 4 P.M. this when the cyclist orderly of Billets + it seemed to myself + Adjutant under 2 hours at the least. Only 2 Coys billeted at RENINGHE. The other two Coys had to be supplied proceeding to HAZEBROUCK. Orders last day were received from Hours 3.	

Army Form C. 2118.

WAR DIARY
or
INTELLIGENCE SUMMARY.
(Erase heading not required.)

Hour, Date, Place	Summary of Events and Information	Remarks and references to Appendices
BILLETS Nº OUDERDOM FEB 12th	All quiet not ceased any return to trench.	
7pm	Received orders that emergency period was at an end – but that all battalions of Brigade when in billets would always be ready to turn out at an hours notice.	A/
FEB 13th	All quiet. O/C 2nd & O/C British ordered to Lt. O'Meer in & through a loophole gun course.	
	Very wet day. – Number of Casualties to date amongst the 2 Junior 8 hundred hours in Trenches 11 killed & 30 wounded.	A/
10 PM	No officers killed or wounded. All quiet.	
FEB 14th		
11 AM	Brigadier General Commanding 84th INF BDE met all Commanding Officers of Battalions at Lyppek Regt Headquarters.	A/
FEB 15th		
3·40 AM	Received orders from BDE HQ to move at once to YPRES	A/
3·50 AM	Sent Rangers to Bays to move at once & rendezvous on VLAMERTINGHE road.	
6·30 AM	Batt HQ moved off with A + B Coy + 1 Stone Transport	
8·15 AM	Batt HQ. A + B Coy + 1st Line Transport arrived Infantry Barracks YPRES	
9 AM	C + D Coys arrived at Infantry Barracks YPRES Brigr Barr HQ of Bn on arrival.	B/

WAR DIARY
or
INTELLIGENCE SUMMARY

(Erase heading not required.)

Army Form C. 21??

Hour, Date, Place	Summary of Events and Information	Remarks and references to Appendices
YPRES FEB 15th 8.30 P.M.	Battalion marched out of YPRES to 3rd Middlesex Regt in Trenches West of Canal. Relieved the 3rd Middlesex Regt in Trenches in Bry Dieu STAFF and up to wait in water roughly in N Trench. B Coy under Capt Hoad-Baron were led wrong by guides & taken right up to loose entanglement of German Trench. Capt Hoad-Baron brought the Coy back into N trench met only 2 casualties. C.S.M. Nannan wounded and Lt D.K. Faris military wounded. Then other of which a few lower cast.	
FEB 16th	Capt Jourdain C Coy sent to relieve O Trench found this trench ⅔ full of Germans this he opened verbally & asked for more troops as his line all been expended. (O trench had previously been captured from Middlesex Regt by the Germans but in our taking over they reported that it had been reoccupied by the Buffs on the night of 15/16 — the fact upon we relieved ——) Putting men here from C Coy his L/Cpl Ashton who was sent up to let trench & reoccupy. 2 platoons under Capt C.S. Nelson in support by signal were needed. C Coy was ordered up to make an attack on O Trench to Canal but owing to day being broken their we received that an attack would be unaware to bring to bring Ladders from fire at 11 A.M. Capt Hoad-Baron be under going to ladders gun fire at 11 A.M. Capt Hoad-Baron N Trench informed that O Trench had been captured by Germans at dawn.	£3
FEB 17th 2 A.M.	Two Coys Cheshire Regt under Major then Bde Head guards entrenched by a chaps to regain a trench in front of that held by D. Coy known as P. Trench, but owing to strength of German position and	£3

Form/C.2118/11.

Army Form C. 2118.

WAR DIARY
or
INTELLIGENCE SUMMARY
(Erase heading not required.)

Instructions regarding War Diaries and Intelligence Summaries are contained in F. S. Regs., Part II. and the Staff Manual respectively. Title pages will be prepared in manuscript.

Place	Hour, Date	Summary of Events and Information	Remarks and references to Appendices
YPRES.	FEB 18th 2 A.M.	Machine gun fire, the attack failed. The 2nd Northumberland Fusiliers who were waiting for the attack by Globe Rgt to take place, to make an attack on O Trench to neutralise it, did not make the attack.	
		Relieved in Trenches by 2nd Northumberland Fusiliers and handed to them in KRUISTRAAT. Casualties during preceeding tours in Trenches Capt F.W. Wood Martin, Capt P.C. Harris, Lieut D.N. Forbes, Lieut C.F.B. Smith and 19 other ranks killed. Capt F.S. Agar, Capt J.A. Campbell, Lieut F.C. Gay, Lieut A.G. Payne & 53 other ranks wounded. Captain K.M. Fair down Lieut F. Mayley & 2nd Lieut H. Biggs and 11 other ranks ill. Capt B.S. Walker & Captain E.S. Ashton admitted Hospital Sick.	See appendices 6 & 7. 211+243.
KRUISTRAAT	FEB 18th	2 killed	
	FEB 19th	Orders received to relieve 2nd Northumberland Fusiliers in same section of Trenches as before.	
	11.45 P.M.	Headquarters & Companies arrived at Railway Dugouts WATERLANDHOECK. Parties proceeded to relieve Trenches.	
	FEB 20th 3.30 A.M.	Relief of all Trenches completed. O Trench was occupied by the enemy.	
	4.35 A.M.	All correct. Enemy have put Large light over us in O Trench.	
	10.30 A.M. 12 NOON	Our artillery opened fire with Lyddite on Enemies Trenches. Telephone communication with Bde HQ broken down.	

1247 W 3299 200,000 (E) 8/14 J.B.C. & A. Forms/C. 2118/11.

Army Form C. 2118.

WAR DIARY
or
INTELLIGENCE SUMMARY
(Erase heading not required.)

Instructions regarding War Diaries and Intelligence Summaries are contained in F. S. Regs., Part II. and the Staff Manual respectively. Title pages will be prepared in manuscript.

Hour, Date, Place	Summary of Events and Information	Remarks and references to Appendices
FEB 20th		
2.45 P.M.	Rifle fire very slight, nothing to be seen from Batt. H.Q. reported to Bde H.Q.	
9.45 P.M.	Telephone communication re-established with N Trench.	
10.15 P.M.	Maxim gun in N Trench out of action.	
FEB 21st		
12.30 A.M.	Lt Harrison + Garrison N Trench relieved by Lt Ward + an equal number. Given orders to support Crowston of Trench CT's impossible to keep open owing to caves in it.	
6 A.M.	Report to Bde H.Q. all correct. Parapet N Trench falling in.	
7.45 A.M.	N Trench being shelled from O. ask for artillery support	
7.50 A.M.	Artillery open fire.	
8.35 A.M.	Shells dropping directly in German parapet	
8.45 A.M.	Two shells 50 yards short	
8.50 A.M.	fire shells short	
8.53 A.M.	shells short	
9 A.M.	Artillery fire stopped as shells dropping nearly into our own trench N	
1 P.M.	German working party working the right of @ Tunnel towards P. Trench. Reported this to Bde H.Q.	

1247 W 3299 200,000 (E) 8/14 J.B.C. & A. Forms/C.2118/11.

WAR DIARY
or
INTELLIGENCE SUMMARY

(Erase heading not required.)

Army Form C. 2118.

Instructions regarding War Diaries and Intelligence Summaries are contained in F.S. Regs., Part II. and the Staff Manual respectively. Title pages will be prepared in manuscript.

Place	Hour, Date	Summary of Events and Information	Remarks and references to Appendices
	FEB 21st 2 A.M.	Orders for our Relief by 4th Royal Fusiliers received.	
	9.15 A.M.	Lieut. SALMON 1st Field Regt brought L-Bair Hip dangerously wounded in head. Went on by Field Hospital.	
	11.50 P.M.	Relief of all Trenches completed. Casualties during 48 hours Officers Nil. Other Ranks 6 killed, 28 wounded.	
	12. M.N.	Batt Hq. left for YPRES Infantry Barracks.	
	FEB 22nd	Battalion remained in Infantry Barracks YPRES, orders received that 84th & 85th Bdes moved from to BAILLEUL next day & come under order of 2nd Division.	(3)
	FEB 23rd 6.30 A.M.	Started to proceed to BAILLEUL by road route. 100 sick went had feet sheltered in YPRES under Lt. R. Ricse M.O.	Tpe no part of Fifth Div (3)
	12. NOON	Batt arrived BAILLEUL & went into Billets. Lt-Col A+B Wallace took over Command of Batt from Capt Rice. Capt R. Knotchbull-Hugessen K-Hospital. Capt. H. Mas assumed Command of Battalion. Strength of Battalion marching into BAILLEUL. 12 officers (including Lt-Col Wallace) & 455 N.C.O men.	(3)
BAILLEUL	FEB 24th	L Battn at BAILLEUL drawing 120 trek men at L R Ricse M.O. arrived from YPRES in Moth lorries.	(3)
	FEB 25th	Lt-Col A.B Wallace resumed Command of Battalion. Bdr Genl Ross also taking over new Command of the Brigade.	(3)

1/7A.

1247 W 8290 200,000 (E) 8/14 J.B.C.&A. Forms/C. 2118/11.

WAR DIARY
or
INTELLIGENCE SUMMARY

(Erase heading not required.)

Army Form C. 2118.

Hour, Date, Place	Summary of Events and Information	Remarks and references to Appendices
BAILLEUL FEB 25th	Lt Col Clissold Commanding 2nd Battalion slipped Reps & Lieut Nelson's Army Adjutant 2nd Battalion left us for to ELITE to meet the 1st Battalion. Lt Williams was proceeding home on 8 days Leave.	F1
FEB 26th	Capt Annesley Hoppers Regt Joined himself for duty relieving from appointment as Bde Ladies Gun Officer 8th Inf Bde. Lt Ladhury whom joined Battalion for duty [Posted to Coys as under.]	
	Lieut Wm HUGGAN 3rd Suffolk Regt Joined to D Coy
	Lieut H.C. HODGES Dorset Regt " B Coy
	Lieut G. BARGH Hants Lancaster Regt " C Coy
	Under orders received previous day the Battalion prepared for a keen of duty in Trench area near WULVERGHEM.	F1
2 P.M.	Ammunition Carts from Cab slightly wagons under 2 Lieuts R. Gallwey proceeded by direct Route to DRANOUTRE.	
4 P.M.	The Battalion met remainder of Transport proceeded by March Route via NEUVE EGLISE to BULL FARM at ROMARIN, relieving 1st DORSET REGT.	
8 P.M.	Arrived BULL FARM. delayed in NEUVE EGLISE owing to Rebels in Him. NEUVE EGLISE owing to EAST SURREYS being off to Trenches. This let him headed out of the Locality in NEUVE EGLISE that afternoon. Battalion left in reserve in Front of at 10 P.M. Rides Night & day Transport while in arrived at BILLETS at DRANOUTRE	

Army Form C. 2118.

WAR DIARY
or
INTELLIGENCE SUMMARY

(Erase heading not required.)

Instructions regarding War Diaries and Intelligence Summaries are contained in F.S. Regs., Part II. and the Staff Manual respectively. Title pages will be prepared in manuscript.

Hour, Date, Place	Summary of Events and Information	Remarks and references to Appendices
BUS FARM. FEB 28th	All quiet, a few Aeroplanes about. A man reported lost night as a suspicious person was arrested, he being identified as a German belonging to Battery of Artillery stationed close to BUS FARM.	
12 NOON	Our guns situated close to BUS FARM doing a lot of firing.	
6 PM.	Brigadier General Potts CB DSO Commanding 84th Inf.Bde. visited BUS FARM. Everything quiet.	

84th Bde.
5th Div.

WAR DIARY.

1st SUFFOLK REGT.

MARCH

1915.
....

Attached:-

Operation Orders.
....

Army Form C. 2118.

WAR DIARY
or
INTELLIGENCE SUMMARY
(Erase heading not required.)

Instructions regarding War Diaries and Intelligence Summaries are contained in F. S. Regs, Part II. and the Staff Manual respectively. Title pages will be prepared in manuscript.

Hour, Date, Place	Summary of Events and Information	Remarks and references to Appendices
BUS FARM — MARCH 1st	All quiet during the day.	
6.15 P.M.	A draft of 58 men from 3rd Batt. Suffolk Regt arrived under 2 Lieut Cherrington Essex Regt.	B
MARCH 2nd 1 AM	Heavy heavy gun fire from our aft. Some distance off, lasted for about 2 hours during which time it was very ... C.O. & Coy Commanders visited the trenches we are going to relieve.	B
MARCH 3rd	All quiet during day	
6 P.M.	5 officers reported for duty having been posted to 3rd Battalion: 2nd Lieut R.G. Purland " L.C. d'Albiac " T. Moore " G.P. Wordley D.F. Gorse-Hodge	
7 P.M.	Battalion Headquarters Staff left BUS FARM & proceeded to Batt Hd in Trenches taking over D Sector from 2nd Cheshire Regt	
8 P.M.	Companies moved up in Trench formation (left BUS FARM & proceeded via DAFFLING FARM) X RF FARM where guides of 2nd Cheshire Regt met them and guided them to the various trenches.	B

WAR DIARY or INTELLIGENCE SUMMARY

(Erase heading not required.)

Army Form C. 2118.

Instructions regarding War Diaries and Intelligence Summaries are contained in F. S. Regs., Part II. and the Staff Manual respectively. Title pages will be prepared in manuscript.

Hour, Date, Place	Summary of Events and Information	Remarks and references to Appendices
8.45 p.m.	Batt. HQ. Staff arrived at Batt HQ. RIBOW FARM.	
10.25 p.m.	Reliefs all round complete	
11.30 p.m.	Officers patrol which was sent out from 12 trench at 7pm by 2nd Lieut. Pigt. did not return — Cpl. Arnold returned who kept a sharp look out for him from our HQ himself.	B
MARCH 4th 4 A.M.	Telephone communication by means of Regimental Telephone established between 11t trench 9./12.S. Bn Ch.	
10.53 A.M.	Battalion HQ. being shelled by enemy's artillery. No damage.	
9.10 P.M.	A patrol consisting of Sergt Buxton + Pte Does returned. Having gone out after dark in front of 12 trench, no clear up position as to supposed sapping by enemy. Patrol reported not that our own seems the supposed sap about 150 yards from our lines + 30 yards from the German lines. They could hear the Germans talking + were soon moving about in their trenches. The supposed sap was only an old damaged communication trench, running back to the German lines and was about 15 feet deep in one width. No signs of sapping + running could be discerned, nor could they hear anything suggesting Brigade very pleased with patrol intelligence to improvements on front out above.	B

WAR DIARY or INTELLIGENCE SUMMARY

(Erase heading not required.)

Army Form C. 2118.

Hour, Date, Place		Summary of Events and Information	Remarks and references to Appendices
IN TRENCHES	MARCH 5th 1.30 AM	A rapid fire for about 10 mins was opened on right of our trenches by our troops probably Queen Victoria Rifles. Came information Numbers of men probably trying to make the German circuit from firing that trench British uhlan had been rather unwelcome. C.O. visited trenches 18, 13 S & 19	
	2.45 AM	All quiet during the day. No 8833 Pte J Besneux killed. No 8880 2nd W Roope and No 4498 Pte D.A. Beck badly wounded yesterday. Conroy today No 8209 P.O. Codling slightly wounded.	
	7.10 PM	2nd Lieut 1st Somerset Regt came into trenches this evening for instruction in charge of some members of 3rd Somerset Regt. C By in support relieved by B By in the trenches.	
	7.30 AM	Lt O.T.C. (Ainur Pitre) came into trenches for instruction (to return). A number of officers 83rd Field Bde visited trenches	84
MARCH 6	2.45 AM	C.O. visited trenches 18. 12.3. 11.3. & No 5 C.P.	
	6 AM	Very heavy artillery fire to North from the Westward.	
	11.30 AM	Counter fire from heavy howitzer by enemy apparently from direction of Lille.	87

4/12

Army Form C. 2118.

WAR DIARY
or
INTELLIGENCE SUMMARY
(Erase heading not required.)

Instructions regarding War Diaries and Intelligence Summaries are contained in F.S. Regs, Part II. and the Staff Manual respectively. Title pages will be prepared in manuscript.

Hour, Date, Place	Summary of Events and Information	Remarks and references to Appendices
MARCH 6th 12 NOON	FRENCHMAN'S FARM about 2½ miles away shelt on fire by shells fired by enemy, a large quantity of 2.3.3 SHR exploded by fires	B
	all quiet sunny day.	
MARCH 7th 2.45 AM	GO DOCTER 13.8.13 IN WAR DIARY	
10.45 AM	Reconnaissance persons received a few shells from enemy. 20 damage.	
7.15 PM	Brigade HQ & 2 Bns YORK & LANCASTER REGT arrived at Brigade Headquarters & the men.	
11.30 PM	all trenches relieved by York & Lancaster Regt.	B
BAILLEUL MARCH 8th 2.30 AM	Battalion arrived at BAILLEUL went into Billets for	C.
BAILLEUL MARCH 9th	a few days rest.	C.
BAILLEUL MARCH 10th	L. Biller	C.
" 11th	L. Willits	C.
" 12th	L. Willits	C.
" 13th	L. Willits	C.
	Lt Willits Lt Col H Clifford DSO Commanding 2 Batt Suffolk Regt.	D

WAR DIARY
or
INTELLIGENCE SUMMARY.
(Erase heading not required.)

Army Form C. 2118.

Instructions regarding War Diaries and Intelligence Summaries are contained in F.S. Regs., Part II and the Staff Manual respectively. Title pages will be prepared in manuscript.

Hour, Date, Place		Summary of Events and Information	Remarks and references to Appendices
BAILLEUL	MARCH 13th	Capt Willson of No.1 2nd Batt Lippard Regt was over from LA CLYTTE to point us.	
"	8 P.M.	Received orders that the Battalion would leave Sunday Monday January 14th to take up a new line of trenches just E. [South]	[1]
"	MARCH 14th 12.1 A.M.	Received orders that Battalion would arrive at 10 P.M. 14th inst	
"	10 A.M.	Battalion left BAILLEUL [by Bus? route] & proceeded to trench area near PLOEGSTEERT to relieve the 2nd Seaforth Highlanders that evening. [Battalion went into Trees farms - the Grand Munque, & the Piggeries for teas etc.]	
NEAR PLOEGSTEERT	8 P.M.	C.O. & Officers Commanding Companies went into the Trenches	
"	8 P.M.	Orders received but to carry out the relief but to stand bye ready to move at a moments notice. Very heavy Artillery fire caused to lose in Malines in a Artillery direction towards ST ELOI.	[2]
"	11 P.M.	Relief definitely cancelled.	
"	MARCH 15th 11 A.M.	Batt Genl Bois & Major Walford were soon out by Bde master Batt P? heard that heavy fighting had taken place at ST ELOI. Germans had captured a certain number of our trenches.	[3]

WAR DIARY
or
INTELLIGENCE SUMMARY.
(Erase heading not required.)

Army Form C. 2118.

Instructions regarding War Diaries and Intelligence Summaries are contained in F.S. Regs., Part II and the Staff Manual respectively. Title pages will be prepared in manuscript.

Hour, Date, Place	Summary of Events and Information	Remarks and references to Appendices
NEAR PROGSTEERT MARCH 15th	Last that enemy attacks were being made with signal guns but already been partially retired. Relief moved forward rate of exit Lainput by the 2 Leinster Highlanders by ourselves. Relief concealed.	
4 P.M.		
5 P.M.	Relief move to take place & to commence at 6.15 P.M. tonight.	
5.45 P.M.	Battalion paraded. Return in living turn meal, & proceeded to relieve the 2 Leinster Highlanders guides met Coys at Hyde Park Corner. 'guides' Coy? to take particular modes. Headquarters Staff went to white Lodge relief is the Park-bay HQ 95 & Burning Barton. Relief completed.	
8.30 P.M.		
11 P.M.	Coy proceeded to HQrs & Inn of Battalion HQ - Leinster Farm. Quiet in the trench line.	
TRENCHES MARCH 16th		
5 A.M.	CO. arrived at Bay Headquarters.	
5.30 P.M.	all quiet during day. No casualties up to 12 noon. No 7676 Pte W. Burns D Coy killed. 9. S.W. No 7853 " G. Hibst " D " wounded. 9. S.W. No 8178 " E. Busch " D " wounded. G. S.W.	ℬ

Army Form C. 2118.

WAR DIARY
or
INTELLIGENCE SUMMARY.
(Erase heading not required.)

Instructions regarding War Diaries and Intelligence Summaries are contained in F. S. Regs., Part II and the Staff Manual respectively. Title pages will be prepared in manuscript.

Hour, Date, Place	Summary of Events and Information	Remarks and references to Appendices
TREVENTES MARCH 16th		
8 P.M.	Battalion HQ shifted to Seaport Farm for the night	
9 P.M.	CO inspected A & B Coys trenches & 1st Camp trenches all quiet	
12 M.N.	Runner received H.Q. B.n arrived the relieved by a unit of the 10th Bn Royal Inf 17/18 " & Battalion would march to Billets in BAILLEUL.	B
MARCH 17th (ST PATRICK'S DAY) 4.30 A.M.	Battalion H.Q. moved down to White Lodge.	
4 A.M.	Pts Curtis Received.	
	Orders received for and Relief to Royal Irish Fusiliers to commence at 10.30 p.m. tonight.	
8 P.M.	No Q^t Farnan A Coy. very slightly wounded in head not admitted to hospital. & the three last stragglers left.	B
MARCH 18th 2.30 A.M.	Battalion left White Lodge having been relieved in trenches.	
BAILLEUL 6.15 A.M.	Arrived BAILLEUL where Billets.	B

WAR DIARY
or
INTELLIGENCE SUMMARY.
(Erase heading not required.)

Army Form C. 2118.

Hour, Date, Place	Summary of Events and Information	Remarks and references to Appendices
BAILLEUL MARCH 19th		
9 AM	Orders received that 84th Inf Bde would relieve the 4th Bde in Trenches opposite KEMMEL. 2nd Cheshire Regt & 2nd Northumberland Fusiliers moved up into Trenches tonight. Sherwood Foresters & Queen Victoria Rifles to remain in Billets at BAILLEUL for Present.	✓
3 pm	Bde HQ moved to LOCRE.	✓
MARCH 20th	L. BELLIS.	
8 PM	Orders received to move to over DRANOUTRE.	✓
MARCH 21st	Battalion left BAILLEUL & proceeded by March route to their bivouacs in BAILLEUL — DRANOUTRE ROAD arriving there at	✓
	4.30 pm. L. Fuchs resting. Officers Commanding Coys went over trenches actn F.	✓
DRANOUTRE MARCH 22nd	— ditto " —	✓
" 23rd	— ditto " —	
" 24th	Battalion went a Coy of the 1st Monmouthshire Regt (T.F) attached to duty relieved 2nd Cheshire Regt in Trenches Sector F.	✓
" 25th	Battalion headquarters KEMMEL CHALET KEMMEL. L. Fuchs.	✓

WAR DIARY
or
INTELLIGENCE SUMMARY.
(Erase heading not required.)

Army Form C. 2118.

Instructions regarding War Diaries and Intelligence Summaries are contained in F.S. Regs., Part II. and the Staff Manual respectively. Title pages will be prepared in manuscript.

Hour, Date, Place	Summary of Events and Information	Remarks and references to Appendices
TRENCHES MARCH 26th	Lt. Hankin.	B
MARCH 27th	Lt. Amelio. [Batt: Headquarters moved at 10 PM to LINDENMEER CHALET]	B
MARCH 28th	Relieved in part by 1st Cheshire Regt. relief completed at 11 PM. Battalion marched back to billets on huts near DRANOUTRE	B
	Casualties during march 24th – 28th.	
	Killed 1" + nil. No 18127 Pte Pepworth D Coy	
	Wounded 25" Lieut H.P. Leroy A Coy.	
	1" No 8093 Pt Gutman A Coy.	
	No 8470 " Brun B D Coy (killed in hospital)	
	62/3 " Lawrence C Coy.	
	6669 C.S.M. Bush D Coy.	
DRANOUTRE MARCH 29th	2 killed	B
MARCH 30th 5:30 PM	1 killed	B
	Battalion proceeded by March went to PACK HORSE FARM + dug communication trench up to FIR TRENCH E2 N.E. BETR.	C Mont K 4. W 1 + 11
	Battalion returned to billets at DRANOUTRE at 2 am 31st inst.	
MARCH 31st	Casualties during digging on opara? No 9327 the Kemp C Coy killed over DRANOUTRE	B
	No 16209 Pt Jordan E C Coy.	
	38th killed NW. Wambeck.	

OPERATION ORDERS.

1st Suffolk Regt.   Copy No 1.
Operation order No 2.
                     Battalion HQ
                     25/8/15

1. The fire trenches and Supporting Points will be relieved tonight by the above Coys.

2. On Rations arriving tonight they will be issued & carried on the man. Trench stores will also be issued & carried up by Coys into the trenches.

3. B Coy Suffolks will relieve D Coy Suffolks in trenches F2 & F6

   D Coy Monmouths less 1 officer & 50 men in SP2 will relieve C Coy Suffolks in F4.

   B Coy Monmouths will relieve A Coy Suffolks in F5.

   A Coy Suffolks will send 1 officer & 50 men to SP3, relieving 1 officer & 50 men B Coy Monmouths who will go into F5.

5

4. Machine Gunners & Telephone operators will remain in trenches & supporting points.

5. A Coy less 50 men, C Coy & D Coy will come into Billets in KEMMEL.

6. Water Bottles will be filled before leaving billets by Relieving Coys. A water cart will come round.

7. B Coy Monmouths will take up rations for 50 men going into F5 from SP 3

B Coy Suffolks will take up rations of 50 men of A Coy & leave them at SP 3 on way up.

8. Guides for all drafts will be at KEMMEL Cross roads at 8 p.m. & will be picked up by Coys on way out.

9. Rations for M Gunners & Signallers will be taken up by B Coy Monmouths for F5, D Coy Monmouths for F4 B Coy Suffolks for F2 & D Coy Monmouths

for SP 2.

10. The written morning reports will be sent by orderly to reach STORE FARM (between SP 2 & SP 3) by 4 AM punctually where an orderly from Battalion HQ will collect them.

           Don Baldwin Capt
            adj 1 Suff R.

issued at 1 PM.
Coys in Trenches informed by Telephone.
Issued verbally to Reserve Coys.

1st Suffolk Regt   Copy No/ 7
Operation order No 3.

Battalion HQ
26/3/15.

1. The fire Trenches and Supporting points will be relieved tonight by the Reserve coys commencing as soon after transport arrives as possible.

2. All water bottles will be filled from water carts.

3. D Coy will relieve F2 & F6
C Coy will relieve F4.
A Coy will relieve F5.
B Coy Supports will send 1 officer & 50 men to SP 2.
B Coy Monmouths will send 1 officer & 50 men to SP 3.

4. Remainder of B Coy Supports & the Coys of Monmouths will go into billets as HETRAMEL.

5. Rations will be issued before leaving billets & carried on man.

6. Trench Stores will be issued from Carts by SergtMajor to Coys before they leave on road between Bn HQ & Band Stand.

7. A Coy will take up rations, in Sandbags for 1 off + 50 men, Monmouths, + leave it at SP3.
+ for 1 off + 50 men in F5.
also for 7 MG + 2 Signallers Sappers in F5.
(also 2 Signallers SP3)

C Coy will take up rations in Sandbags for 7 MG + 2 Signallers in F4.

D Coy will take up rations in Sandbags for 1 off + 50 men also 7 MG + 2 Signallers + leave at SP2
also for 7 MG + 2 Signallers F2
+ 2 Signallers F6.

Coys after drawing rations & storing them will be ready to move up to get Trench Stores etc when told.

Coys must ensure that their orderlies know where STORE FARM is. this morning only two written reports turned up there, the orderlies having all lost their way, this must not occur again

8. There will be no guides for coys

issued at 2p.m.

J.A.Baldwin Capt
Adj, 1/4th R.

Brig. telephone to Trenches & S Ps.
Kirkaldy to relief coys in Bedlets.

1st Suffolk Regt.   COPY NO 1. 10
Operation Order No 4.

                         Battalion Head Quarters
                              27.3.15

1. The Firing Trenches and Supporting points will be relieved by the Reserve Coys tonight commencing as soon as possible after rations and stores have been moved.

2. Water bottles will be filled from Water Carts.

3. B Coy Suffolks will relieve D Coy Suffolks in F2 & F6

   D Coy Monmouths will relieve C Coy Suffolks in F4

   B Coy Monmouths will relieve A Coy Suffolks in F5.

   A Coy Suffolks will send 1 officer & 50 men to SP 3 to relieve 1 officer & 50 men B Coy Monmouths there.

   C Coy Suffolks will send 1 officer & 50 men to SP 2 to relieve 1 officer & 50 men of B Coy Suffolks there.

4. 1 officer + 50 men B Coy Monmouths, A Coy Suffolks less 1 officer + 50 men & C Coy Suffolks less 1 officer + 50 men will on relief march to Billets at LINDEN HOEK CROSS roads.

    B Coy Suffolks
1 officer + 50 men now in SP2 will join their Coy in trenches F2 + 6.

5. B Coy Monmouths will carry up rations in Sandbags for 1 officer + 50 men A Coy Suffolks and ~~2 officer~~ Signallers (garrison of SP 3) & deposit them at stone FARM.
They will also take up rations for 9 Machine Gunners & Signallers in F5.

D Coy Monmouths will carry up rations in Sandbags for 1 officer + 50 men C Coy Suffolks & 9 Machine Gunners & Signallers (garrison SP2) & deposit them outside SP2. They will also take up rations for 9 Machine Gunners & Signallers in F4.

B Coy Suffolks will carry up rations in Sand bags for 1 officer + 50 men B Coy Suffolks joining them in fire trenches from SP2

12

also rations for 2 Signallers in F 6. I
rations for the 4 Machine Gunners & Signallers
in F 2.

6. Rations of men going up to relieve from
billets will carry three days rations on them.

7. Coys will move off in following order
(1) B Coy Lysachs
(2) D Coy Dromouths
(3) B Coy Dromouths
Trench stores will be drawn by Coys from
Carts on road between Batt HQ + Band Stand.

8. Batt. Headquarters will be moved from
here about 9.30 pm tonight to LINDEN-
HOEK CHALET.
Coys in Trenches who are being relieved &
coming into billets, will come to LINDEN-
HOEK cross roads, where their new billets
will be shown them.
Dressing Station will be at LINDENHOEK
Cross roads.

9. Morning Reports will as usual be sent to
STORK FARM punctually at 4 AM.

10. There will be 20 guides for Coys
    relieving.

                    D.B. aedm Captain
                    Adjutant 1st Supp R.

Arrived at 2 pm.

Bay Telephone to Coys in
Fire Trenches & Supporting Points.

Infantry to Reserve Coys.

14

1st Suffolk Regt.   Copy No

Operation Order No 5.

Battalion Head quarters.
1. 4. 15.

1. The Battalion will take over sector F trenches from 2nd Cheshire Regt tonight

2. Starting point Entrance A & B Coys Billets, facing Dranoutre on the DRANOUTRE — BAILEUL Road 6.30pm.
order of march.
   Batt Headquarters.
   B Coy.
   D Coy
   A Coy
   C Coy
   Transport.

3. Dress. Marching order. Great coats.

4. Rations for 2nd April will be issued before leaving Billets and carried on the man.

5. Trench Stores will be issued at LINDENHOEK cross roads & taken up to the trenches by Coys manning trenches

6. Distribution of Trench Garrisons.

B Coy F2 70 men F4 40 men F6 50 men.

D Coy F4 60 men F5 100 men.

A Coy SP 3   50 men.

Reserve Coys.
  A Coy less 50 men LINDENHOEK FARM.
  C Coy   HANNAT FARM.
Officers of both Coys will go to HANNAT FARM.

7. B Coy will detail 1 N/c + 6 men as "gangers" to work in "Regent Street" & keep it in good order. These men will be permanent during tour in trenches. This party to have gum boots.

8. D Coy will detail 1 N.C.O. & 12 men to report at Quarter Master's Stores at 5.30pm to accompany wagon to draw 4 webs of wire netting & 1 roll plain wire from Bde Hq & take up to North End of F5 where RE are going to erect a breastwork to connect with ward. B Coy will furnish the party with a guide.

9. C Coy will detail 1 officer + 50 men

will march in rear of battalion and on arrival at LINDENHOEK cross roads will draw floor boards & take them to SPY FARM where they will be met by 2 RE who will assist them in laying floor boards in REGENT STREET. This party will ~~also~~ take gum boots & put them on at SPY FARM.

10. A Coy will detail 1 Officer & 20 men to roof the Dug outs SW of SP2 close to Bridge over STUIVERBEEK. The Pioneers will accompany this party to assist.

11. Blankets will be drawn by Reserve Coys at LINDENHOEK ~~cross roads~~. Officers should make a small bundle of Blankets etc for men who on reserve. They will all be sent to HANNAT FARM.

12. Guides from Cheshire Regt will be at LINDENHOEK cross roads at 8.15 AM.

S M Baldon Capt
Adj 1 Loyd R.

28th Division.
84th Brigade.

The 84th Bde rejoins 28th Division from 5th Division – 6/4/15.

WAR DIARY

1st SUFFOLK REGT.

1st – 9th April

1915

WAR DIARY
INTELLIGENCE SUMMARY.
(Erase heading not required.)

Army Form C. 2118.

Remarks and references to Appendices: **1st Suffolks**

Hour, Date, Place	Summary of Events and Information
BILLETS NEAR DRANOUTRE	
APRIL 1st	
5.30 pm	Battalion proceeded by motor buses to LINDENHOEK to take over trenches "F Sector" from 2nd Lincoln Regt.
11 P.M.	Relief of trenches completed. B + D Companies in the trenches + supporting points, C + A Coys in Reserve + Farm at LINDENHOEK.
APRIL 2nd	In trenches all quiet
APRIL 3rd	In trenches all quiet
9 pm	Fire trenches + supporting points relieved by Norfolk Coys C + A. B + D Coys came back in Reserve. Los system of the 7th Batt Nth + Sthy Regt (T) came into trenches on the night of 2nd/3rd April also 3rd April.
APRIL 4th	
11.30 pm	7th Battalion North + Suthy Regt (T) arrived to relieve us in F Sector. Relief not completed till 4 a.m. April 5th owing to many los streams of returning Battalion + then Machine Gun section setting out on way up to the trenches.
APRIL 5th	
6 AM	Battalion arrived in Huddens in hopes near DRANOUTRE.

WAR DIARY
INTELLIGENCE SUMMARY.
(Erase heading not required.)

Army Form C. 2118.

Hour, Date, Place	Summary of Events and Information	Remarks and references to Appendices
BILLETS NEAR DRANOUTRE	Casualties during tour in trenches April 1st – 4th, 2 K, 3 W	
	No 3894 Pte Mason C. D Coy killed	
	No 9753 Pte Snow " " wounded	
	No 9093 Pte Bolland H. C Coy wounded	
	No 5650 Pte Hippo W. C Coy killed	
	No 8977 Pte Baker A. E Coy wounded (reported previously)	
APRIL 6th	L. Builo	
APRIL 7th	Battalion inspected with the rest of 84 Infantry Brigade by Lieutenant Genl Davies in field near LOCRE.	
APRIL 8th	Pte General Bols CB DSO Comdg. 84th Infantry Bde inspected all drafts which joined Battalion since arrival & number of Buesto. Lienyt 18 officers 116 other Rank's.	
APRIL 9th	L. Builo. The following Complimentary order received.	

28th Division.
84th Brigade.

WAR DIARY

1st SUFFOLK REGT.

9th - 31st May

1915

WAR DIARY

INTELLIGENCE SUMMARY.
(Erase heading not required.)

Army Form C. 2118.

1st Suffolks

Hour, Date, Place	Summary of Events and Information	Remarks and references to Appendices
Sunday May 9th 5 p.m.	The following officers & draft arrived. Capt R.D Rushbrooke, W.H. Mackay 2nd Lt Parsons, Lockett, Dykhoff & a draft of 127 N.C.Os & men, from Falaclare via Havre & Rouen, and marched outside POPERINGHE on the road to Ypres, met by Q.M Lt Godbolt & Lt Hogan Transport Officer. Lt Venning with 29 men survivors from the trenches & Q.M. & Transport Staff in fact.	
Monday May 10th	Reports to the Brigade Officer re following officers wounded & missing Lt Col L.B Wallace Missing Captain D.V.M Balders Wounded " R.Chalmers " & missing " F. Ellis " & missing Lt C Bundle Wounded & missing 2/Lt G Harwood To Hosp sick " R.O Pargiter Missing " E Barth " " C.P Hornby " " S Winch " " K.H.G Cayley " 2/Lt D.Bean Missing Other ranks 391. A few stragglers reported during the day The batt was reorganised under the command of Capt R.D Rushbrooke Lt Venning 2nd in command & Lt Mackay Adjt Asst Adjt The survivors of the Battn were refitted.	Approximately missing

WAR DIARY
or
INTELLIGENCE SUMMARY.
(Erase heading not required.)

Army Form C. 2118.

Hour, Date, Place	Summary of Events and Information	Remarks and references to Appendices
Monday May 10th 6pm	Orders received to parade for trenches, which was cancelled	
9pm	Order to move at once to huts via Vlamerting [Thuk NW 9 Ypres] D camp; arrived 12.30 am	
Tuesday May 11th	Awaits orders. Artillery was active on both sides. German shelling of Ypres with incendiary shells during the day. S. side of Ypres was set on fire.	
5pm	Orders were received to return back to camp outside POPERINGHE that night.	
	The Battn. marched back behind the Northumberland Fusiliers, Welsh & Cheshires. The remainder of the 84 Brigade.	
9pm	Arrived at camp & bivouac there tonight & awaits orders. On arrival at the camp Capt. Ready & Lt. Nott Taylor & 2/Lt. Hastings 3rd Batt. Suffolk Regt. joined the Battn. & were taken on the strength	
	The town of POPERINGHE was shelled that night for a short time. There was guns.	
Wednesday May 12th	Capt. Ready took over command from Capt. Ruxton. The 84 Brigade consisting of the Northumberland Fusiliers, Welsh, Cheshire & Suffolks are formed into a Composite Battn. & awaits orders to move at once with transport	
5.30pm	Orders received for the Composite Battn. to move to Abele	

WAR DIARY
INTELLIGENCE SUMMARY.
(Erase heading not required.)

Army Form C. 2118.

Instructions regarding War Diaries and Intelligence Summaries are contained in F.S. Regs., Part II and the Staff Manual respectively. Title pages will be prepared in manuscript.

Hour, Date, Place	Summary of Events and Information	Remarks and references to Appendices
Wednesday May 12. 9pm	The Composite Battn. is billeted in farms 3 miles S.W. of POPERINGHE To rest & await orders. Suffolks billeted in farm H.33 up to this date the total strength of his 1st Suffolk Regt. is 11 Officers including D.M. O'Neill and 286 N.C.O.s + men, attached to H. Menos Detachment.	
Thursday May 13.	Bath awaits in brit. A, R.E. Engs. under command of Major Rea Whittle + 3 Officers moves to Farm H.2.5. 150 I.O.R.'s E.9 H.33. Headquarters + Req. remain at Farm H.33.	
5:30pm	Wol. Payne Ready to move at once.	
6pm	Maj. Hay cork D.S.O. arrives at H.Qu. & to take on the strength. Maj. Maycock D.S.O. takes over command of Battalion from Capt. Rowley. I Orders arrived from 84th Inf. Bn. Lieut. P. Suff. at 11am + 12 W. on to form a Composite Brigade under command of Brig. J.f. Bols C.B. D.S.O. II The remaining under Offs. (places) under Maj. F. Hay cork D.S.O. Commany, and a staff Officers from 28th Division will in such (unit). III Troops under Maj. Hay cork D.S.O. will move by motor bus to HERZEELE in accordance with allotted order. Approx 1st Monmouth. IV On meeting 12 County Division.	

WAR DIARY
INTELLIGENCE SUMMARY.
(Erase heading not required.)

Army Form C. 2118.

Instructions regarding War Diaries and Intelligence Summaries are contained in F.S. Regs., Part II and the Staff Manual respectively. Title pages will be prepared in manuscript.

Hour, Date, Place	Summary of Events and Information	Remarks and references to Appendices
Friday May 14th 8.30 am	Orders issued by Bn HQ to 11th Manchesters & 12th London for relief of 11th & 12th London withdrawing van of the cross roads N of Wormhoudt L17.3 Rly Shed 27 at 1 P.M. Order of march — 1st Rifles 12th London 1st Manchesters	
2 P.M.	Head of Column will be immediately PW of the cross roads in L.17.b. Strength of 11th Suffolks at this date 19 officers 225 other Ranks 12th and m. move by motor bus to HERZEELE 1st m.ch. Transport following. Coln via WATTOU arriving at 5 P.M. ROAD to WERMOUDE Suffolks billeted in village on the ROAD to WERMOUDE C+D Coys billeted in the school. A+B Coys billeted in FARM 150y/s.	
6 P.M.	W.O.s club Officers Officers Mess Village Town Hall. H.Q. Village Town Hall. Companies are placed at the disposal of O.C. Companies from 9 a.m. OM/7am over at 7 a.m. JR WG on the Road to WERMOUDE. A+C Coys one billet in the Farm. Officers in charge of Companies at their disposal. A.C.G. Capt PD Ramshotham. Reg't P Hammy CSgt 271 Inkster Sgt 271 Hutchins by Liberty arrived from the area and posted to No 5 Coys.	
Saturday May 15th 9.30 p.m.	A.D. rof (12) reinforcement 156 NCOs + men and are taken in the strength of the Batln.	

(73989) W.4141—463. 400,000. 9/14. H.&J.Ltd. Forms/C. 2118/10.

Army Form C. 2118.

WAR DIARY
INTELLIGENCE SUMMARY.
(Erase heading not required.)

Instructions regarding War Diaries and Intelligence
Summaries are contained in F.S. Regs., Part II.
and the Staff Manual respectively. Title pages
will be prepared in manuscript.

Hour, Date, Place	Summary of Events and Information	Remarks and references to Appendices
Sunday May 16th 10 am	Battalion paraded to march into Bus Priers, w/Jun WO & B Coy Relieved	
9.30 am	Inspection of troops by Commanding Officer	
Monday May 17th	Strength of Battalion from this date 12 Officers and 2 OR	
10.30	Battalion parade. Marching order.	
Tuesday May 18th	Companies are placed at the disposal of Officers Commanding Companies.	
Wednesday May 19th	Companies are placed at the disposal of Officers Commanding 2nd Bn. Reveille 3rd Suff. Regt attached to the Regt. Visit to the fields; Enemies to day and have been taken on the Tonight.	

WAR DIARY
INTELLIGENCE SUMMARY.
(Erase heading not required.)

Army Form C. 2118.

Hour, Date, Place	Summary of Events and Information	Remarks and references to Appendices
Thursday 20/5/15	Lieut S Bradley rejoined from Hospital (Rouen) & is taken on the strength.	
Friday 21/5/15	Companies paraded at 9 am the disposal of the C.O. for purposes of Commander's Inspection from 9am.	
12 pm	The Field Marshal Commander in Chief will inspect the Battalion at 6 o'clock in HERZEELE SQUARE. Troops to parade in 11.45am	
	The Field Marshal Commander in Chief arrived in Cars, finished Inspection, French 5th Brigade & addressed the Battalion. Congratulating it	
12.15 pm	on their fine fight at the 2nd Battle of YPRES, adding that their great success as a regiment was won though untold hardships — owed and on the part of had which they would not have done it without.	
2 pm	Received orders from Bde HQ to billets at 94 OR arrived	Lieut & Transport
8 pm	ABEELE from Furnes 2.30 pm	
	Draft arrived at billets to details companies under orders Lieut C.J. Taylor	
		2 to E Coy in Cwat
		2 - F Coy Lt Northop
		2 - T Packam

Army Form C. 2118.

WAR DIARY
or
INTELLIGENCE SUMMARY.
(Erase heading not required.)

Instructions regarding War Diaries and Intelligence Summaries are contained in F.S. Regs., Part II and the Staff Manual respectively. Title pages will be prepared in manuscript.

Hour, Date, Place	Summary of Events and Information	Remarks and references to Appendices
Saturday 22/5/15	Orders B4/14 Brigade will move to a billeting area W of VLAMERTINGHE in accordance with march table. 1st line Transport 1 Bayonet Coln of Train will accompany Battn. Billeting officers will meet Staff Officer at the Xrvs R36 at 9.0 d.a. 4 pm Mad March 1st Monmouth 1st Suffolks 2nd Cheshires 2nd Northumberland Fusiliers Battn to bivouac.	
12.55 pm	Company outside HQs.	
1 pm	Battn move off attg. Strength of battn up to this date 128 Offrs 2870 R has billets for the night & awaits orders	
8 pm	Battn billeted over an area of dire	
Sunday 23/5/15	Battalion rested by Church parade	
12.15 pm	Received orders to stand by	
Monday 24/5/15 3.45 am	Orders to move with Transport HIND Eq VLAMERTINGHE	
6.15 am	Transport moves off li ho SH Q twine BDC is attack the munchies who truds	
12.30 pm	Battn marches away independently thinly h YPRES & Vlamer a e was crossing railway going up over railway	

WAR DIARY or INTELLIGENCE SUMMARY

Army Form C. 2118.

(Erase heading not required.)

Hour, Date, Place	Summary of Events and Information	Remarks and references to Appendices
24/7/15 5 p.m.	Between ZILLEBEKE and the pond, working up to his G.H.Q. line, from if attack, Cheshire + Northumberland Fusiliers in the firing line. Monmouths in support; Suffolks in reserve. Arrived at G.H.Q line, a few casualties on the way. The plan of the attack as received from his Bde was with Major Haycock OC 1st Suffolks, who is at present missing. Further orders re attack	
3.30 p.m.	Germans who hold the church, SE of LAKE nr HOOGE are being attacked by a platoon. Above IIBA north edge. Said to be holding late still holding HOOGE. Our casualties are believed to be slight. Suffolks will move direct out on right of village. Keefer's patrol to Menin Road. 9/- Welch will take the Germans above mentioned in flank. GKQ line running from bridge on railway I.10.D to ZILLEBEKE Village to GKQ line now called SWITCH in support in town chy, an attack from South in direction of HOOGE probably at 4 p.m. attacking troops have packs in charge of 1 man per Company.	

WAR DIARY
or
INTELLIGENCE SUMMARY.
(Erase heading not required.)

Army Form C. 2118.

Hour, Date, Place	Summary of Events and Information	Remarks and references to Appendices
Monday. 24/5/15. 6 p.m. In the Field.	**The attack.** The 1st Suffolks were ordered at about 8.30 p.m. 24.5.15. and at the commanding officers request, moved up in line along the hedge at I.17.d. and Menin Road to the Field I.15.a. The Regiment started the attack. that number was considerably lowered by losses inflicted though still well under 400 Rifles strong, and received between 4 p.m. and 6 p.m. while maneuvering to take up position. The 1st Suffolks faced Bayonets, and proceeded in good order into the attack. Within about 150 yds. from the enemies position the order to charge was given by the Commanding Officer (Major F.W.O. Maycock D.S.O.) who himself led the Regiment until the line was released by heavy Rifle and Machine gun fire from the enemies twenty, that he was forced to fall back to the edge of the field (I.11.b in front of the enemies position (I.11.d) While defying this position the Commanding Officer reviewed the situation and decided to fall back and reorganise his command at I.17.b then to repeat at Brigade Headquarters, and the Regiment awaited the order to launch the second attack.	Valuable information was obtained by 2nd Lieut S. Bradley and Lieut Kemble who carried out reconnaissance under the fire of the enemy. Both these Officers are at present missing. All Map References refer to Belgium Sheet 28 1/40,000.

WAR DIARY
INTELLIGENCE SUMMARY.
(Erase heading not required.)

Army Form C. 2118.

Instructions regarding War Diaries and Intelligence Summaries are contained in F.S. Regs., Part II and the Staff Manual respectively. Title pages will be prepared in manuscript.

Hour, Date, Place	Summary of Events and Information	Remarks and references to Appendices
Sunday 25/7/15	During the day stragglers kept coming in to the Bat H.Qrs in PK9 trenches giving further & details of situation in the morning which a few men.	
12.10 pm	Heavy shelling during the morning over the trenches towards YPRES. Orders Batt HQ are moving to CRUCIFIX at LILLE GATE of YPRES and all reports to C mammoth in trench (no 3 car) level crossing on road and time here 8 telephone wires to BtHQ are mounted in trench 1/16 wire is therefore. Have heavy hostile in railway cross is there by us and lay that half WHITTEPOORTE FARM in field by us by main. hills by C~ mourn. Reply moving BtHQs note. No further comms in the later evening in com...	
4 pm	Orders received from Bde HQs that B Coy will relieve Qth Bde HQ and forms of C & D R Br from R Bigod to southern of WHITTEPOORTE / railway on billets W of VLAMERTINGHE on withdrawing to (onward) (on relief) (officers 2 offrs & 20 ORs of R Bn) (except mounted R) wise companies of 3"B" & aa junction N C O's by	

(73989) W.4141—463. 400,000. 9/14. H.&J.Ltd. Forms/C. 2118/10.

WAR DIARY
INTELLIGENCE SUMMARY
(Erase heading not required.)

Army Form C. 2118.

Hour, Date, Place	Summary of Events and Information	Remarks and references to Appendices
24/5/15. 11:45 P.M.	Maj. Haycock received orders f/ 10th Bde HQrs C/o roads at ZILLEBEKE. Brig. Genl Bols DSO. gave orders that the remnant of the Brigade must retire (incs. at once + launch an attack on the German line, finding 400yds. The Ry.Bde would be supporting in the Centre + Right of the line. Frontage from White Bridge extreme right- WHITTLE POORTE FARM + Y's. MENIN ROAD. Bellew ade farm. Enemy were supposed to be in WHITTLE POORTE FARM. This FARM was to be taken at all costs. Suffolks position in the extreme My. C + D. Companies in the 8th Line. A + B in support. Farm when taken at all costs. 8th Coy. The attack to commence.	
25/5/15 12:30 a.m.	The Battle won (and up 1740 + moved off in June B + D Coy. leading into Menin Rd from there North Forward Old WHITTLE POORTE FARM facing East. The Welch Ryts bey on the left duringth in with R O Y L I on right Batt'n in Ord. Orders were given to fix bayonets and advance. We advanced to within 60 paces of the wood reformed in the Sunken Rd in front Enemys Position. The Welch Ryts (2 Coys) being Rd in on the left.	

WAR DIARY
INTELLIGENCE SUMMARY.
(Erase heading not required.)

Army Form C. 2118.

Hour, Date, Place	Summary of Events and Information	Remarks and references to Appendices
25/5/15 12.30 am (Allied Crs)	Officer in charge hay haycock DSO D.C. 1st Tuffs leads the charge bravely and almost immediately a murderous fire was opened by the enemy with M.G. + rifle fire from S.S. Corner of wood. An also an enfilade fire from S.S. Corner of wood. The men were moved down to muster accordingly but 2nd Lieut Packard with C.S.M. Pye + 6 men of the Tuffs succeeded in driving the Prussian in in the S. corner of the wood where they were joined by details from the Rifle Bde (mostly attaching 100 men). Lieut Packard was killed. The Prussian alongside by him and the Germans. 26/5/15 Day of inward work where hard work march ??? ?? during the attack 24.4.25.6. Lieut W.M. Hoyworth YPRES Maj. Haycock DSO } 24.4.25.15 Lieut & QM Graham to 9.16.5. Pte Back himself 2nd Lieut Packard Regt S.M. Crane 7.0.5.15 Gpl Allen C.S.M. C.Q.M. Pye S.R. Pegg Lieut & Asst M.O. 7422 Goldhawk 4268 Pte Swann for excellent work 7-5-19 Sgt Griffiths throwing during the war 4257 Pte Bartle	

(73989) W.4141—463. 400,000. 9/14. H.&J.Ltd. Forms/C. 2118/10.

WAR DIARY
INTELLIGENCE SUMMARY
(Erase heading not required.)

Army Form C. 2118.

Hour, Date, Place	Summary of Events and Information	Remarks and references to Appendices
25/5/15	Push that BILLEGATE I 14 a at 6.4.5 pm today near Kind 9/5/4 in BOE will in rly on ready railway line is H.12.D. W9 YPRES (where they will join it's ready mammoth R.) will be in place by another another will attack move to railway siding and collect all packs and equipment belongs to those that been in four GS wagons which will bring him R and W9 railway crossing at F.30 pm see memo on R. will there march then $\frac{2}{3}$ to BULLI WEST of VLAMERTINGHE	
9.30 pm	Battalion 26 officers and 942 ORs. marched of to VLAMERTINGHE then to YPRES.	
26/5/15 Wednesday 1 am	Arrived at our Bivouac W9 VLAMERTINGHE. Remained in Camp. Awaits orders Capt had have arrived to relieve on his strength & took over command of Battn. May have DSO. Nothing more of the attack.	

WAR DIARY

INTELLIGENCE SUMMARY

Army Form C. 2118.

Hour, Date, Place	Summary of Events and Information	Remarks and references to Appendices
Wednesday 26/5/15	Return showing Casualties among Officers & OR. Major Hayes DSO missing Capt R D Rushton the lt + minor, Lieut S Brady to hospl. Kemble killed Lieut C Taylor & Lieut Willaby wounded, 2 Lieut E Hartopp & F Hammond sick & Lieut Martin missing. Other Ranks wounded to Rouen 37, wounded 91, missing 5 sick 135. OR including sick numbers returned for hundreds Officers & unlucky MO OR 230. Strength of Battn. Transport 2/116 in. and 385 ORs. unlucky 1 Dr. 1 Ammunn. 1 ASC Command. Recmmd attch. B4 th Bde will move more round HERZEELE today as details of tpt will be ready tomore at 11 a.m. from divisional train transport and/9/14. Arrives at Ram at tpt will more with Battn at Billeting parties Battn will move with (off) Capt at HERZEELE SQUARE at 2/3 m will meet the staff morn 9/1. Via POPERINGHE + HOUTKERQUE	
Thursday 27/5/15 12.30 a.m. Friday 28/5/15 "12 pm"	Suffolk Battn moved HERZEELE took over some billets en bivouac	

WAR DIARY
INTELLIGENCE SUMMARY

Army Form C. 2118.

Hour, Date, Place	Summary of Events and Information	Remarks and references to Appendices
Saturday 29/5/15 1:30 a.m.	Draft of 89 O.R. arrived from the Base & were taken on the strength & posted to companies. This draft composed of many of the original "Battn" who came out in August & were wounded slightly & are one company for the A & C Coys. Lieut Bray under 2/Lt Dunlop. Another one Company under Lieut Heaton Venning for D Coy & therefore only centures places at the disposal of Officers Commanding Companies from 9 a.m.	
3:30 p.m.	Lieut Heaton Venning home from leave & reports to Adjutant. Officers Commanding companies inspected the Base and said a word to every man in the 2 Coys & visitors from leave. Then that is the 3 C & D Coys. The Col. has a good deal to say to men of his Command.	
Sunday 30/5/15 11 a.m.	Companies placed at disposal of Officers Commanding Companies from 9 a.m. Church Parade for Bat. in HERZEELE SQUARE.	

Army Form C. 2118.

WAR DIARY
or
INTELLIGENCE SUMMARY

(Erase heading not required.)

Instructions regarding War Diaries and Intelligence Summaries are contained in F.S. Regs., Part II. and the Staff Manual respectively. Title pages will be prepared in manuscript.

Hour, Date, Place	Summary of Events and Information	Remarks and references to Appendices
Monday 31/5/15	Companies placed at the disposal of Officers Commanding from 7.15 a.m. The following Officers arrived (& have been taken on the strength) the Battalion & posted to Coys. Capt H Hannay to B Coy & will take over command from Lieut Kenny. 2/Lt G H Bar " " " " C.F Wright " A " " IC Hollinrake " A " " DL Salis	

"A" Form.
MESSAGES AND SIGNALS.

Army Form C. 2121
No. of Message ____

Prefix ____ Code ____ m.	Words	Charge	This message is on a/c of.	Recd. at ____ m.
Office of Origin and Service Instructions.	Sent			Date ____
	At ____ m.		Service.	From ____
	To			
	By		(Signature of "Franking Officer.")	By

TO 2/Suffolk

Sender's Number.	Day of Month	In reply to Number	
BM 24	24		AAA

Germans who broke through S. of lake near HOOGE are said to be holding a position about I.18.a, north edge aaa Our cavalry are believed to be still holding HOOGE village aaa 2/Suffolk will move abreast and on right of 1/K.S.L.I. keeping parallel to the MENIN road and attack the Germans above mentioned in flank aaa GHQ line now runs from bridge on railway I.10.a to ZILLEBEKE village aaa former GHQ line is now called SWITCH aaa No moves to occupy SWITCH aaa 27th Division is launching an attack from Sanctuary in direction of HOOGE probably after 4pm aaa Attacking troops to learn faces in charge of 1 man per company.

Stilton Capt BM.

From 2th Inf Bde
Place
Time 3.30 p.m.

The above may be forwarded as now corrected. (Z)

Censor.   Signature of Addressor or person authorised to telegraph in his name.

"A" Form. Army Form C. 2121.
MESSAGES AND SIGNALS.

| TO | 1/Suffolk | | |

| Sender's Number. | Day of Month | In reply to Number | AAA |
| BM 53 | 25th | | |

Bde HQ are moving to casemate nr LILLE GATE YPRES aaa send all reports to O.C. Monmouth in trench just E of level crossing nr I.10d aaa Have now had a telephone run to Bde HQ aaa Have we any troops in railway wood I 11 d aaa is the report true that half WITTEPOORT FARM is held by us and half by Germans aaa Reply early.

Eastwood Capt BM

84th Inf Bde
12.10 pm

To
Bde Maj.
84th Bde.

Your change of H.Q. position noted,
I also order re reports.

I can give no information regarding
Wilte Poort Farm & Railway Wood.

I am at present in G.H.Q. trenches
with 30 stragglers of last nights
engagement.

My report herewith giving as
much information as I know of.

A/Adjt
Suff. Regt.

"A" Form.
MESSAGES AND SIGNALS.

Army Form C. 2121.

Prefix	Code	m.	Words	Charge	This message is on a/c of		Recd. at	m.
Office of Origin and Service Instructions.			Sent			Service.	Date	
			At	m.			From	
			To					
			By		(Signature of "Franking Officer.")		By	

TO — Suffolk

Sender's Number.	Day of Month	In reply to Number	A A A
* BM 57	25%		

Eighth Brigade will relieve eightyfourth Bde and portion of eightieth Bde from South end of WITTE POORT farm to railway aaa Battalions on relief will return to former billets west of VLAMERTINGHE aaa Each Battalion (except monmouth R) will send two officers or NCO's to guide companies of eighth Bde aaa guides to be at LILLE gate I.14.a at 6.45pm today aaa Units of 84½ Bde will on relief march by railway line to Asylum H.12.d west of YPRES where they will find tea ready aaa monmouth R. will not be replaced by another unit but will at dusk move to railway cutting and collect all packs and equipment belonging to 84½ Bde and load them on four GS wagons which will be on MENIN road west of railway crossing at 8.30 p.m. aaa monmouth R. will then

From Place
Time

The above may be forwarded as now corrected. (Z)

Censor. Signature of Addressee or person authorised to telegraph in his name.

* This line should be erased if not required.

"A" Form.
MESSAGES AND SIGNALS.

Army Form C. 2121.

Prefix	Code	m.	Words	Charge	This message is on a/c of:	Recd. at	m.
Office of Origin and Service Instructions.			Sent		Service.	Date	
			At	m.		From	
			To				
			By		(Signature of "Franking Officer.")	By	

TO

Sender's Number.	Day of Month	In reply to Number	A A A

march to their old billets west of VLAMERTINGHE aaa Acknowledge.

E.F. Mon Capt B.M.

84th Inf Bde

4.30 pm.

From
Place
Time

The above may be forwarded as now corrected. (Z)
Censor. Signature of Addressor or person authorised to telegraph in his name.
* This line should be erased if not required.

Regimental
SM Chase   Has done with marked
   excellent [?] under very difficult
conditions round YPRES

Sergt Pery   very [?] excellent work done
   by the trenches in the 2nd Battle of
YPRES

Pte Evans
Lce Cpl Nash   Removing wounded under
Pte Clarke   very heavy shell fire
Sergt [?]   during the 2nd Battle of YPRES
Cpl Tuck

9165 Pte Backhouse   Highly recommended
   for bravery in carrying out messages
   under heavy shrapnel fire & bringing
   wounded to reconnoitre

"A" Form. Army Form C. 2121.
MESSAGES AND SIGNALS.

Prefix	Code	m.	Words	Charge	This message is on a/c of	Recd. at	m.
Office of Origin and Service Instructions.			Sent		Service.	Date	
			At	m.		From	
			To				
			By		(Signature of "Franking Officer.")	By	

TO: 1st Suffolk Regt.

| Sender's Number. | Day of Month. | In reply to Number | AAA |
| BC 143 | 27 | | |

84" Bde: will move to the billeting area round HERZEELE tomorrow aaa Battalions will be ready to move at 11 a.m. aaa Detailed orders will be issued at 8 a.m. aaa First line transport and baggage Section will move with Battalions aaa Billeting parties will meet the Staff Captain at Herzeele Square at 2 p.m. aaa Acknowledge

Wyndhoper Lt
T.O. 1st Suffolks
12.20 PM

From 84" Infty Bde:
Place
Time 11-46 pm

Capt.

28th Division.
84th Brigade.

W A R   D I A R Y

1st S U F F O L K   R E G T.

June

1 9 1 5

WAR DIARY
or
INTELLIGENCE SUMMARY

(Erase heading not required.)

Army Form C. 2118.

Instructions regarding War Diaries and Intelligence Summaries are contained in F. S. Regs., Part II. and the Staff Manual respectively. Title pages will be prepared in manuscript.

Hour, Date, Place	Summary of Events and Information	Remarks and references to Appendices
1st June 1915	Return of Reinforcements joining 3/1st May 1915" Officers:— Capt H Hanney 3" Suffolk Regt. 9 Lieut. Ve Hollenrake Temporary R R Ross Commission L Salis attached 1st Suffolk Regt of Wright	
2nd June 1915 3rd June 1915	Capt Hanney took over command of A. B. Coy from Lieut Venning. Companies are places at the disposal of Officers Commanding Companies are places at the disposal of Officers Commanding Companies are places at the disposal of Officers Commanding reveille to dinner hour.	
3 pm	Commanding Officers Parade for Route March. "A" Coy, with Posse the Starting point — Shoppers head in Hergate Square at 3 pm. Marches to trenches at WYLDER Places Relieving trenches for instruction. Strength 9 Batln Parade total 180 Officers 4 9 2 O.R including 4 2 O.R on command at POPERINGHE R.A.M.C. 86" 3/2 Indian fare a concert to the Brigade in the trenches behind the Hospital.	
6 pm	Companies are placed at the disposal of Officer's Commanding.	
4th June 1915 6 pm	The Despatch Riders on out Parry "will give an exhibition tournament" in Hergate Square.	

Army Form C. 2118.

WAR DIARY
or
INTELLIGENCE SUMMARY

(Erase heading not required.)

Instructions regarding War Diaries and Intelligence Summaries are contained in F. S. Regs., Part II. and the Staff Manual respectively. Title pages will be prepared in manuscript.

Hour, Date, Place	Summary of Events and Information	Remarks and references to Appendices
5th June 1915	Companies are placed at the disposal of their Coys Command. Capt. R.M.P. Reid have assumed command of the Battn in accordance of May 1915. Lieut. J.H. Shackney took over the duties of Adjutant of the Battn on the 9th May 1915. A Diary of 107 M.G. reinforcements joined the Battalion on the 4th June 1915 sent to Tahta on the Tsingtu. R.C. wouldn being sent jointly by R.A.M.C. & "Ryker" & London will adhere in Tahta in the Tahta Union HERZEELE Church	
	11am Parade for Divine Service at 11am in HERZEELE SQUARE	
6th June 1915	Companies were placed at the disposal of Officers Commanding	
7th June 1915	2pm Officers Commanding their respective Battn at 2 pm. 8pm O.C. Coys went with the Commanding Officer to the trenches at WYLDER, to arrange relief of trenches at night (1 intended purpose only) A & C Coys (less of 2 pattern) to trenches Battn machine staff returned	
	8.30pm R.D. Coys returns. Maj. J. Smellon Shenson being arrived for duty on 6th June 1915 assumed Command of the Battalion accordingly. With references to despatches as the Battn H.Q. Coys Orpadies & Drummers.	

WAR DIARY or INTELLIGENCE SUMMARY

Army Form C. 2118.

Hour, Date, Place	Summary of Events and Information	Remarks and references to Appendices

7th June 1915

Officers and details to Empannes are under.
A Coy. Lieut. P.E. Hunt, 2 Lieut. J.C. Littlewood, 2 Lieut. 1 Gold,
Reg. Lieut. 2 G Fleming. 2 Lieut. B.H. Rea, C.Wright, H. Littmann.
C Coy. Capt. H. Hannay, 2 Lieut. S.P. Wallop, G. West.
D Coy. Capt. H.M. Reade, 2 Lieut. E.M. Rapp, T. Prestwich.
Head Quarters Officers Major L. Sneddon, Johnson Capt. N.R. Madden
Lieut & Adj. I.H. Shackley, Lieut & Q.M. Bryan, Lieut A.M. R. Goatorn
2 Lieut C.E. Lovatt. 2 Lieut G. Pearson M.G. Lieut J. Picard M.O. RAMC
2 Lieut H.P. Bluwn, training amongst (on duty, in N.M.) men in Gallery
at W. Knight. Companies commenced from "A" list Ripa.

Proceeding to Battn. 208/1545. 5970 R's.

8th June 1915

Companies employed at the disposal of Officers Commanding.
Capt. Meadows was on leave to England. Relieved on 13th inst.
Companies employed at the disposal of officers Commanding of
Bury Battalion. Company Commanders were arranged to avoid
as far as possible our movement in the sun between the hours of
11 am and 4 pm. Training of this nature itself takes place between the
Platoon 1 dusk or before Breakfast.

6.30 pm

C. Coy. Battalion was sent to practise relieving trenches, in conjunction with the
Cheshire Reg. (Came over early to Post. Rendezvous (corners)

WAR DIARY
or
INTELLIGENCE SUMMARY.

Army Form C. 2118.

(Erase heading not required.)

Instructions regarding War Diaries and Intelligence Summaries are contained in F.S. Regs., Part II. and the Staff Manual respectively. Title pages will be prepared in manuscript.

Hour, Date, Place	Summary of Events and Information	Remarks and references to Appendices
9th June 1915	A Class [?] demonstrated that [?] of Ophthalmic [?] when proper precautions are taken. [?] is on the SW @ Line 9.6 (Third 28)	
2 pm	2:30 pm —	
1 pm	28 [?] + 6 NCOs left 13 inclu[?] train from Base H.Q. 1 pm to attend.	
6 pm	R.A.M.C. Est 2 off 21 mm [?] for a month [?] duty.	
10th June 1915	Brigade Route march — Men paraded at 5.30 am — marched & rode in Brigade as Transport — Brigadier expressed himself to the C.O. as very pleased with the men's marching & praised the appearance of the Transport. Unit reached Base an hour before [?] packs & 10 men for Coy — parades of 10 men for Coy — Ms received orders for move tomorrow 2 pm.	
11th June 15	Bn. left Wenzel [?] marches to Rosenhill. Arriving 7.30 pm. Went into huts — Bivouacs for n/c. 2 of. Person left at Wenzel under Medical Orders. Lt. C.M. Gwynn & Draft of 127 NCOs & men joined Bn. at Rosenhill & taken on strength.	

Army Form C. 2118.

WAR DIARY
or
INTELLIGENCE SUMMARY.
(Erase heading not required.)

Instructions regarding War Diaries and Intelligence Summaries are contained in F.S. Regs., Part II. and the Staff Manual respectively. Title pages will be prepared in manuscript.

Hour, Date, Place	Summary of Events and Information	Remarks and references to Appendices
12 June 1915.	Bn. Paraded, finishing Skirmishing, marched off to take over following trenches from Rifle Brigade in neighbourhood of St Eloin. A.Coy. L.t Hunt. T20 Mortar B3, B2 & P3. fire trenches B - " Fanning & 91. M.G. - - - Pu, R2 & P2 - 1P2 & support T. C - " Capt Harvey 1700 - - - Pu, & P2 - Support T. D - (Capt Rooby, N. Staff R. Etsham) 8.commander of H.Q. Coys in support in Ridge Wood.	
13th June 15.	Bn. HQ at the Brasserie - Shrivel Week - N. Franklin. Relief of Rifle Brigade & Bn. Completed 4.40 am - 10 a.m. O.C. H.C. 171nb. Enemy mining under P3. Reminder all quiet - N.E. front. 12 noon - Casualties reported - Other Ranks, 1 wounded. 5 pm. O.C. S. Coy report Enemy suspected mining towards P4 & P5 5pm. Counter mine started & Nt in P3. - Enemy reported point down attr. Counter mine in P3. ready at 9pm. but failed to explode - Casualties for 13 noon = O.R. Ranks 3 wounded. Capt Needham Moored B. from leave	
14 June 15.		

Army Form C. 2118.

WAR DIARY
or
INTELLIGENCE SUMMARY.
(Erase heading not required.)

Hour, Date, Place	Summary of Events and Information	Remarks and references to Appendices
15 June 15.	G.O.C. Div: with Brigadier visited B̄n H.Q. Trenches. Casualties 5-12 noon - O.Ranks 1 Killed 1 wounded. 6 p.m. Situation quiet. N.E. wind. Report from O.C. H.Coy. party (6-6½ a.m.) German to Latin Trench. Officer & P3. Three of their enemies in Khaki, one in dark blue. 2TC looked acting Signalling Officer. P3 has done excellent work in the Tunnel.	
16 June 15.	2 a.m. C.O. visited all four trenches. 2.15 W.Aux Coucl: mine in P3 exploded. Blown in German mine (?) (T.A. Confirmed). Portion of our own Trench.) Casualties 6-12 noon – O.Ranks 1 killed 1 wounded. 12 noon. Situation Normal. Slight N.E. wind. 6 p.m. —	
17th June 15:	12 noon. Situation quiet. Casualties O.Ranks 1 wounded. 4.50 p.m. B̄n H.Q. shelled. about T.K.Q. 200 yds W. & Engrs. 11.15 p.m. Enemy bombed P3 with rifle grenades – wounded 1 man severely, 1 slightly. — X	

WAR DIARY or INTELLIGENCE SUMMARY

Army Form C. 2118.

Hour, Date, Place	Summary of Events and Information	Remarks and references to Appendices
18 June 15	15: M.R. moved to Dugouts 100 yds S.E. of Brasserie. Enfilade rifle grenade fired into P3 causing fatal up recounted. Rifle killing his own ground, two others. Enemy snipers very troublesome - officers F & men splendid - bullet - screens much damaged & thought. 12 noon - Canadian 2 killed 11 wounded, other ranks - 6pm. Situation normal - N.E. wind. 11.15pm. Do. Draft 62 men with ammn. taken on string M.T. 2Lieut. Frantham & Palterman joined 7.15 in afternoon from Artel. Coy.	
19th June N.	11 N. am. Situation normal - Casualties 6 1/2 noon. O/ranks 4 wounded. 4.73.(Illus winch min.) Coy returned from Trenches, places to Reserve at Ridgewood. C & D. except front & support trenches.	
20. June N.	Situation unchanged - Returned from P3 riveted. Sap from Enemy Front to front army right 19/20 report no sign of activity - F when funnel arr'd & adjustment made Sap.	

WAR DIARY
or
INTELLIGENCE SUMMARY.
(Erase heading not required.)

Army Form C. 2118.

Hour, Date, Place	Summary of Events and Information	Remarks and references to Appendices
21 June 15	2.30 am. Working party returning from trenches held up in wood. Enemy shell fire. Casualties 1 Killed (wounds) 12 noon. Situation quiet. Casualties no'above. No. 653 CSM Ryan E promoted actg RSM v.o. J Clan from 9th May 15. 11.15 pm Situation unchanged.	Casualties 1 killed (wounds) 2 lieut.
22 June 15	Situation normal. Casualties F2 nen O'Ranks 2 wounded 2 Lieut.	
23rd June 15	Bn relieved by 3rd Bn R Fusiliers 7pm. Casualties reported 7.15 pm — O Ranks 3 wounded.	
24 June 15	2 am — Relief completed — Bn marched to bivouac at a farm 1½ miles S. Dickebusch arriving there 3 am — Day of Rest!	
25 June 15	2 P.M. Affiliation lecture by O.C. Companys	Written by mistake by O. Clerk /MJT
26 June 15	9 am. Short lecture by O.C. on discipline crimes etc. and permitted of military bops placed at disposal of O.C. Coys.	

WAR DIARY
or
INTELLIGENCE SUMMARY.
(Erase heading not required.)

Army Form C. 2118.

Hour, Date, Place	Summary of Events and Information	Remarks and references to Appendices
25th June 1915	9 am Battalion parade at 9 am. Companies marched off and did a little Company drill during the morning. In the afternoon Companies were played at the disposal of Officers commanding.	
26th June 1915	9.15 am Battalion Parade. Marching order without packs. Smoke helmet to be carried. Half Companies practised artillery formation. 10 am - 1 NCO, per Co. paraded at H.Q. 3/w musketry instruction. 1 pm + 1 NCO per Coy paraded, also 1 Officer + 10 and NCOs per Company paraded. Lewis & Packard's/w instruction	
27th June 1915	9 am Battalion Parade. for divine service. 12.30 pm Accident occurred at the bomb throwing class. An unexploded bomb was handed to Lt Packard, who left it NT	

WAR DIARY
or
INTELLIGENCE SUMMARY.
(Erase heading not required.)

Army Form C. 2118.

Hour, Date, Place	Summary of Events and Information	Remarks and references to Appendices
27th Jun 1915	Whilst preparing to throw it a grenade exploded in his hand, wounding him in the knee + hand. Also Cpl Forsdike in the thigh. Both were sent immediately to his field hospital. 6.15pm Battalion paraded + marched to trenches under Capt Heathcote as follows:- A Coy G. N10 + N12. B Coy B, O19 + S7; C O2; D Coy N6. All surplus 2 C.O's + men per company under 2 Lieut Halsey Kilner in reserve + were accommodated in dug outs in RIDGE WOOD. Company Commander reported to O.C. 20 + 13th H Qrs Q1- 5 p.m. + proceeded to trench later on in day light. Trench Bn H 6's in dug outs S04 or X 9 BRASSERIE	

WAR DIARY
or
INTELLIGENCE SUMMARY.
(Erase heading not required.)

Army Form C. 2118.

Hour, Date, Place	Summary of Events and Information	Remarks and references to Appendices
26/June/1915	27th & 28th. 2 a.m. Battalion relieves 1st Welch Regt. 2nd Lieut (Signaller Officer) was heavy wounded about 1 a.m. + walked unfortunately killed by a stray bullet. Casualties up to 12 noon 10 other rank 1 W. O. Rs. A field gun of ours which was emplaced in under arrangements at Gordon's FARM at 11 a.m. fired for the trial of No 896.4 Regt Hume 1st Suffolk Regt No 1748 " W Jagger " " " " " + + + + + + + + + Previous to May R.T. To k. 1st Welch Regt. Members & Captain 2nd Chatham Regt + Lieutenant 2nd Funteris. 7 P.m. 3 yrs detachment was thrown in the B De Causeway WORIDGE WOOD	
28/June/1915	lull 12 noon : Nil Casualties	
29/June/1915	C.O. + Capt Nectham made a visit of the trenches Lieut 1st McNicol R.A.M.C attached 1st Suffolk Regt recommended for military Cross, for excellent work in the field	

Army Form C. 2118.

WAR DIARY
or
INTELLIGENCE SUMMARY.
(Erase heading not required.)

Instructions regarding War Diaries and Intelligence Summaries are contained in F.S. Regs, Part II and the Staff Manual respectively. Title pages will be prepared in manuscript.

Hour, Date, Place	Summary of Events and Information	Remarks and references to Appendices
29th June 1915	Major F.A. White D.S.O. Hynned the Battn.	
30 Jun 1915	Major F A White D.S.O. assumed command of the Battalion. The present Suffolk cemetery by the BRASSERIE has been enlarged & a new one has been made at RIDGE WOOD in conjunction with the 1st Wiltshire Regt & Bryn. Casualties afternoon OR's 1 killed.	F.A.White Major. Command'g 2/Suffolk Regt.

28th Division.
84th Brigade.

WAR DIARY

1st SUFFOLK REGT.

July

1915

Army Form C. 2118.

WAR DIARY
or
INTELLIGENCE SUMMARY.
(Erase heading not required.)

Instructions regarding War Diaries and Intelligence Summaries are contained in F.S. Regs., Part II. and the Staff Manual respectively. Title pages will be prepared in manuscript.

Hour, Date, Place	Summary of Events and Information	Remarks and references to Appendices
1st July 1915	All trenches were visited by CO to day. Situation during the day quiet + unchanged.	
2nd July 1915	Trenches visited by the CO today. Sn. Elm. Thomson & Capt. Mawthorn. Casualties between Officers + other Ranks. 1 Hon P.H. wounded slightly. 3 wounded. Situation during the day quiet. 1 sick. No change.	
3rd July 1915	Trenches visited by the CO during the day. Situation normal. A draft of 18 Officers + 225 OR's joined the Battalion 2nd July 1916. There were taken on the strength. The staff team arrived at 1.7. Give Transport for the night, during the Day were ready to move to them. Companies during the Day. All trenches were visited by the CO during the day. The S.M., the S.M. Situation normal. Casualties OR's. 2 wounded. 1 sick.	

WAR DIARY
or
INTELLIGENCE SUMMARY.
(Erase heading not required.)

Army Form C. 2118.

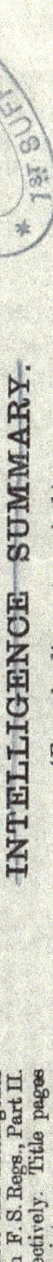

Hour, Date, Place	Summary of Events and Information	Remarks and references to Appendices
4th June 1915	Trenches visited by CO about 1 a.m.; a good deal of rifle fire was kept up by the enemy during the night. Situation during the day normal. Battalion was relieved by the 2nd Cheshire + marched back independently to RIDGEWOOD Hdrs of the Battalion at GORDON FARM. W9 with D Coy, A.B. + Scout. B day into WOOD. Relief was completed at 12.22 p.m. Casualties nil.	
5th June 1915	Capt. Leatham taken over command of B Coy. Draft arrived under Transport with 2 Lieut. H. J. Prentice at 9 p.m. 4th June 1915 + were marched to their Company quarters. 10.30 a.m. CO inspected draft — in the woods, mostly composed of Cavalry Reserve draft. 2.30 p.m. CO (B.B.) left. Trams are infantry Battalion. I saw all officers + N.C.O.s.	

Army Form C. 2118.

WAR DIARY
or
INTELLIGENCE SUMMARY.
(Erase heading not required.)

Instructions regarding War Diaries and Intelligence Summaries are contained in F.S. Regs., Part II and the Staff Manual respectively. Title pages will be prepared in manuscript.

Hour, Date, Place	Summary of Events and Information	Remarks and references to Appendices
5th June 1915	Details 20 officers and 750 O.Rs. from A Coy. as a working party for the 2nd Welsh Regt. at communication trench in BOISCARRE. 8.30 p.m. M.G. Section at work on entrenchment in reserve line between BOISCARRE and West redoubt. Battalion strength including 8 officers and 23 officers & 981 O.Rs. Casualties 8 officers & 1 O.R. wounded & sick.	
6th July 1915	Companies were placed at the disposal of officers commanding companies made day into RIDGEWOOD. During the day Batts and 1st Welsh & 2nd Cheshires at Coy officers hd Qr. 2 sick, 1 wounded.	
7th July 1915	Companies were placed at the disposal of officers commanding. Companies busy during day supervising duty in RIDGEWOOD. D Coy made two covers with them hari BOIS CORDON FARM.	

(73989) W4141-463. 400,000. 9/14. H.&J.Ltd. Forms/C. 2118/10.

WAR DIARY or INTELLIGENCE SUMMARY

Army Form C. 2118.

Hour, Date, Place	Summary of Events and Information	Remarks and references to Appendices
7th July 1915	Casualties. Officers nil. ORs 4 sick. Battalion found working parties for 1st Welch & 2nd Cheshire in the trenches at night. Also completing Brigade Dressing Station by N. side of RIDGE WOOD.	
8th July 1915	Companies placed at the disposal of OC's commanding Front ORs. By one Coy in hospital. Battalion found working party 370 ORs. 3 Officers to 1st Welch, 1 Officer, Findlay & 2 Chishime worked in the trenches. 1st Welch ORs hit. Casualties: Return Officers hit Army Sgt Wraith 1 OR & 1 Sgt army sp.	
9th July	Companies placed at the disposal of Officer Commanding Major J Sinclair Thomson was admitted into hospital today sick. 3 sick ORs. Casualties 10 Officer. Battalion parade for duty 8 Officers 8.45 am Battalion for working parties to the 1st Welch Fusiliers and 250 ORs to work for the 1st Welch. The remainder of the 2nd Cheshire & 1st Welch Battalion was Capt Heathcote and 5 Officers.	

WAR DIARY
or
INTELLIGENCE SUMMARY.
(Erase heading not required.)

Army Form C. 2118.

Hour, Date, Place	Summary of Events and Information	Remarks and references to Appendices
10 July 1915	Work on the defensive line from BOIS CARRÉ to VIERSTRAAT deepen & improving the line. The line to be occupied by whatever Battalion is in Brl. House in RIDGE WOOD Companies placed at the disposal of O Commanding CO went out during the morning to reconnoitre a piece of land N.W. of RIDGEWOOD outside Bn HQs at 2 p.m. Br. Machine Gun Head HQs Lieut O'Gor[man] Head HQs. Sent a working party to Old Bn HQs. 50 yds E of BRASSERIE. 2/Lt Junkison with party of 75 ORs. went out at 8.30 pm to work at further HQ structure. 6 p.m. Lieut O wood hymned his B.Cy. & has taken over the posts. Enemy returning from dural V— is taken on the L.they 15 T/parks & [—] arriving. Also 8 ORs. in M.G. Section. Lt C C3.	

Army Form C. 2118.

WAR DIARY
or
INTELLIGENCE SUMMARY.
(Erase heading not required.)

Hour, Date, Place	Summary of Events and Information	Remarks and references to Appendices
10th July 1915	Situation quiet. Antimony about 9.45 am ho. of an age'd me (casualty return for the 24 hrs.) Ypres hit Strix 18 ock. 2 Lieut Hollinia left to day for Bailleul to undergo a course in machine gun. Officers in machine gun teld are 2 nd Cheshires Common Battalion to Right, no worthy. Bn in hospital at this sup to d y Officers Engineer placed for the disposal of Officers Commanding Battalion have age for the sure a of O.C. in RIDGE WOOD at 3 p.m. Battalion will R.P release 2nd Cheshires tonight. Co. Capt Heath arr. + O.C. Coy came went to Bn. HQ. this afternoon tread the General of Brigade from Thicket to our new Chaw. On the line was occupied by the 63 Bde. Batln with later two three	10th July, huge meaning (ft' acct) was picked up in our lines this morning between 9.33am + 9.140am thought to be that from CO. 2nd Lt. the 69th Bally RFA Simply huge received with many small have exploded the enemy's salving at this by use of its hole. BOISQUARANTE Sans then the were inflict 12 July small rifle 69th Batt. Amunition/supply Timmurying/supply which Krumer + 9 think have been decreaseefoaten in exclusion 0.16a Vig Smoke lbs 607a 11 in to floors sure + adcant has been reported probably on to commence his taken them St. Hushar 2 Lt RFA. 69th Battery RFA.
11th July 1915		

WAR DIARY
INTELLIGENCE SUMMARY

Army Form C. 2118.

Hour, Date, Place	Summary of Events and Information	Remarks and references to Appendices
11/July/1915	Weather tomorrow light. Battalion to remain at Gordon Farm tonight. Situation Quiet. Wdg & estd. Casualties 3 sick.	
12th July/1915	Battn recvd orders to leave Sud'm'r FARM and to take over trenches occupied by the York & Lancs & Northumberland Fusiliers. Coys marches independently and went to their respective trenches. B Coy relieved York 10 Fusiliers in M.I. & M.I.A. trench. A & C relieved the York & Lancs in the L. trench. Two platoons of D Coy were in reserve at VIERSTRAAT, and the other two platoons were in reserve at Batln H.Qrs. were in reserve at Battn H.Qrs. Cross Rds. about ½ mile N.W. of VIERSTRAAT. The Battn recalls GORDON FARM.	

WAR DIARY or INTELLIGENCE SUMMARY

Army Form C. 2118.

ORDERLY ROOM * APR 1915 * 1ST SUFFOLK REGT

Hour, Date, Place	Summary of Events and Information	Remarks and references to Appendices
12th June 1915	At 10.30 p.m. orders left over the new Battn H.Q. The Relief was carried out satisfactorily at 11.30 p.m.	Extract from Sir John French's despatch "Lt-Col Dalrymple-Hamilton commanding the 2nd Battle of YPRES, the 1st Suffolks. This in an attempt to cover a gap in the line & were surrounded & overwhelmed."
12th June 1915	Promotions + Appointments. Extract from the London Gazette war published for information. Temp. Capt's. Commissions Offrs. were made Hon/Lts. March 20th 1915. 2/Lieut J. Roll-Spurrell Reserve. June 9th 1915. Lieut.Henning, + M.I. & B Coy were relieved by the 7th Brigade. The relief was carried out as follows:— B. Coy relieved at 11 a.m. & Coy. completed at 12 o.c. B. Coy + 2 Platoons of C. Coy. marched to "CANADA" Hd: under command of Capt Wood & reinforced the 6th Batt. The other 2 Platoons of C Coy. with Batt. H.Q., 2 Platoons of D. Coy reliev'd D. Coy. Very weak. Both H.Q. & 2 Platoons of D. Coy. with trench mortar A + C Coys histry A + C Coys	@ At 12.25 p.m. the centre of the Bde. from the Battery cross-roads to the Ypres-Menin road was heavily shelled by howitzers, which had been reported by aeroplane shortly before, & were apparently dummies. Meanwhile the Australians withdrew. Three more batts. had been moved up to reinforce 2 Bgr. Bns. when Moulin up in support of General H.Q. line

WAR DIARY
or
INTELLIGENCE SUMMARY

(Erase heading not required.)

Army Form C. 2118.

Hour, Date, Place	Summary of Events and Information	Remarks and references to Appendices
1st July 1915	Orders from the 2nd in Bn in Bayell. The following NCO's were made Captain June 8th 1915 W.M. Kaye c. " " " " " 8 G. Vernon. And the following 2nd Lt's were made Lieut. June 8th 1915. J.O. Houlton. " " " " Q. Hume " " " " J.C. Parsons	
15th July 1915	A & C Coys were returned to the trenches on the night of the 15/16 by the 2nd Batt King Own. During the Relief Bn H.Qs. moved to YORK House. On Completion of relief at 11.20 p.m. Batt. H.Qs. Left. A & C Companies assembled at SANDBAG Villa. B & D marched off under Capt R Westram Billeting area LE WESTOUTRE down. arrived at 3.30 p.m. Very well Batt arrives at billets at 3.30 a.m. (2 Companies famous.) C.O. + adj. rode on in front of the 2 Companies arrived at new Batt. H.Qs. at 4.30 a.m.	

WAR DIARY
or
INTELLIGENCE SUMMARY

Army Form C. 2118.

Hour, Date, Place	Summary of Events and Information	Remarks and references to Appendices
15th July 1915	B Coy + part of D Coy marches under Capt Wood Independently to entrain from CANADA HUT to New Billets.	
16th July 1915	Battalion's and available notes Co + OC Companies took lt Bde HQrs at 9.30 pm to Recce the Bigades & B to find Where there where their own men were. No orders received about moving to the new billets area. Transport moved to LOCRE new Baths HQrs. at 7 pm. Delay am Caused by am from Bde Baths walks more before 7 am DHQ henters Ships Baths. Became too late.	

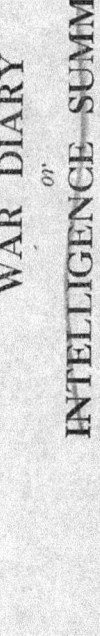

WAR DIARY
or
INTELLIGENCE SUMMARY
(Erase heading not required.)

Army Form C. 2118.

Hour, Date, Place	Summary of Events and Information	Remarks and references to Appendices
17th July 1915	6.15 a.m. Batt. moved from WESTOUTRE & marched to LOERIE & billeted over Res Billeting Area. As usual. Battalion HdQrs.	
18th July 1915	Batt. paraded for Divine Service at 10 am. B Company furnished the fifes & drums & 8.30 pm Fife, Drum, played the service by the Church Company were placed at the disposal of Officers Commanding during the day.	
19th July 1915		
20th July 1915	The Battalion moved from LOERIE to the Trenches at KEMMEL. Moving by ½ Co's. at 25 min. intervals at 6 p.m. C Coy. remained in reserve at KEMMEL School with the surplus from the other 3 Companies. The Co. Commanders arrived at the trenches at 6.20pm & took over the Cantin. on arrival. The reliefs were carried out successfully.	The Battalion returned to the trenches in the S & H trenches. Capt. Busby & Reg. attested the Staff. The Battalion paraded in the 19th Infantry Brigade Reserve to the front.

WAR DIARY
or
INTELLIGENCE SUMMARY

Army Form C. 2118.

(Erase heading not required.)

Hour, Date, Place	Summary of Events and Information	Remarks and references to Appendices

On the morning of July 20th 1915, Battalion HQ's took over the Dozen House & Kemmel from the 2nd Wilts on Completion of Relief 12-40am.

Disposition of the Coys in the trenches. D Coy #3, #4.
A Coy Nos. & sups. H1 & H2. A Coy. #1 & #2. & support trench
A Coy was attached to A Coy. D. Coy 6" trench
5 & 6 OR's from D Coy were attached to O Coy 6" trench
trenches. #3, #4, #5 & were ordered by the O.C. SPKI
Regt' when war was watch he commanded, & the TO. #1 Q Coy.
a supply point on account by #1 to Q Coy.
Situation quiet during the day. Casualties nil.
Co's a patient visit the trenches
between 5 pm & 8.30 pm.

July 21/1915.   The situation has not become very changed from 15
day. Casualties: O.R's 1 killed. A Coy 2 wounded. B Coy.
1 wounded. O.R's 4 S.P. ?.

Certain movement & shelling on the enemy side to the
front is drawn attention. The fire trenches in Trench Screen
were very close to the Sim in our Advance Line. And reasonable
Artillery & any fires over our H1 & H2 front line.

1st Battalion
1st & 2nd
Norfolks

WAR DIARY or INTELLIGENCE SUMMARY

Army Form C. 2118.

Hour, Date, Place	Summary of Events and Information	Remarks and references to Appendices
22nd July 1915	A draft of 16 men arrived from England with three officers. 2 Lieut Rutler Rickards was posted to D Coy & other Supr L/B Coy. The draft of 16 O.Rs. includes 7 signallers, remainder lot O.Rs in reserve problem. Distribution of Staff & companies as unposted. See July report.	See July report.
23rd July	As draft.	
24th July 1915	Lieut Hollamshe completes his M/G course and rejoined his Coy. On the 25th inst 8 F.S.C.M. sentences the following men as follows: No 954 B Platoon 7 & 2 yrs. Imp HL } Sentences " 9234 Volunteer B 10 yrs Imp HL } balance " 9681 " Hallam, 3 months H.L. } to work out sea Lieut Rutler Rickards to an attack (This morning during July report. section for duty. Llewellin, Middles, Skelton in charge.	to work out sea during July report.

WAR DIARY
or
INTELLIGENCE SUMMARY

Army Form C. 2118.

Hour, Date, Place	Summary of Events and Information	Remarks and references to Appendices
25th July 1915	C Coy relieved the 6th Welsh in F3, F4, F4a. SP&I 5 Officers by 10 & 11 OC Coys. Transport & Train H.Qrs.Qpp. were also relieved by 6th Welsh. 2nd Lt. Warnock & an advance party, with the remainder of the Oth Company relieved the 5 seaford KEMMEL. Arrived Bn H.Qrs from Reglandt Office 10 pm & 50 Mrs Bivouacd at KEMMEL at 1 am & war pati [illegible] H.Q.Coy problem.	Daily rep of Battalion diary the Battalion in the trenches. See appendix.
26th July 15.	Officers & Hunt horses came with the Draft.	
27th July 15.	Coy improves Dugts & afterwards Reserve duties. Oth Coy. 2 hour parade were paid a visit by 6 A Coy. The 60 received Lieutenant Thorpe Draft Officers & other ranks mostly the Battalion came out of the trenches. Guide Available Guide	

Army Form C. 2118.

WAR DIARY
or
INTELLIGENCE SUMMARY
(Erase heading not required.)

Instructions regarding War Diaries and Intelligence Summaries are contained in F. S. Regs., Part II. and the Staff Manual respectively. Title pages will be prepared in manuscript.

Hour, Date, Place	Summary of Events and Information	Remarks and references to Appendices
26 July 1915	In the morning the Second & others started Relief was to be relieved, but in the evening the order was cancelled to Relief. Both Place that night. Casualties 2 wounded. Situation Quiet.	See the reference See Daily report Appendices.
27 July.	Situation remained unchanged the second relieved near Fort. The Battalion was to relieve near Fort. The Battalion was to be relieved in the evening at 10 p.m. by the 2nd Shropshires - 9th Manchesters (2) trenches. With one the Shropshires & 1/5 S.R. & 1/8 H.H. just Cashmere trenches Lothbury from the 9/Manchesters. The Relief was completed at 11.40 p.m. & Northumberland Fusiliers both Bgde. D.T. moves from in an interior H.Qs.

WAR DIARY
or
INTELLIGENCE SUMMARY

(Erase heading not required.)

Army Form C. 2118.

Hour, Date, Place	Summary of Events and Information	Remarks and references to Appendices
27th/28th July	Companies on a lath and open lath to LOERE stab on his Rillu, at LOERE HOFF FARM & BADAJOZ HUT. Bn H.Q's known to LOERE Came on report. C.O. and adjutant left Bn HQ's at REMMAISE after the last Coy reported MG HQ's & forwarded to the new HQ's at LOERE took over his Equipment at 9.30 a.m. Battn rested.	
28th July.	Inspection on C.O. 12 noon. C.O. saw all officers afterwards at a conference afternoon. Re Line is care of track. Worked off to reconnoitre the	

Army Form C. 2118.

WAR DIARY
or
INTELLIGENCE SUMMARY

(Erase heading not required.)

Hour, Date, Place	Summary of Events and Information	Remarks and references to Appendices
29th July 1915	Baths visited in the Baths at LOCRE. Baths parade-Men & Officers B+D A+E Huts. C+D Coys at 10 a.m. + A+B Coys at 3 p.m. R+B Lectures in the morning. 1 C.S.O in the afternoon. C.O. + adjutant went round the 4 guards at the cross Roi KEMMEL during the night.	
30th July 1915	3.30 a.m. Received orders to be ready to move at 5 minutes notice. Heavy firing all along the line of Battalion was warned. Battalion ready to move at 4½ + 5 a.m. Wire received (Gas gone) for regiment. Quieter during latter day	

WAR DIARY
or
INTELLIGENCE SUMMARY.
(Erase heading not required.)

Army Form C. 2118.

Hour, Date, Place	Summary of Events and Information	Remarks and references to Appendices
30th July 1915	Battalion paraded at 10 am. It visited by the 19 Officers & 672 ORs. formed up in 3 rows. behind the Bedouin Huts. CO took the parade & thanked the Battalion.	
31st July 1915	Coase & Stalin Battalion has worked partie with mud to relieve the 6th Welsh Ry. at 7.45 pm. at ARCADIA Dug outs. Stanley Power Battalion H.Q.s. 6 days a week. A Co B C D	Much improved health. Medical supplies arrived. Officers transport will be accommodated in On arrival the Battalion will be accommodated in

Army Form C. 2118.

WAR DIARY
or
INTELLIGENCE SUMMARY
(Erase heading not required.)

Instructions regarding War Diaries and Intelligence Summaries are contained in F. S. Regs., Part II. and the Staff Manual respectively. Title pages will be prepared in manuscript.

Hour, Date, Place	Summary of Events and Information	Remarks and references to Appendices
31st July 1915	Orders for "A" Coy will proceed his trenches for two coys in trench & will proceed before the Battalion. 2 hand startup will go on infront. Platoons even shown & the nine day into —	
12. m. n.	Bat'n arrived at extraction of my Coys & Blower. 2nd Bedfordshire and Yorkshire, & but was carried out in good order at about 11 P.M.	

28th Division.
84th Brigade.

WAR DIARY

1st SUFFOLK REGT.

August

1915

WAR DIARY
or
INTELLIGENCE SUMMARY.

(Erase heading not required.)

Army Form C. 2118.

Instructions regarding War Diaries and Intelligence Summaries are contained in F.S. Regs., Part II. and the Staff Manual respectively. Title pages will be prepared in manuscript.

Hour, Date, Place	Summary of Events and Information	Remarks and references to Appendices
August 1st. Alexia Dug-outs	"Minden Day" was spent at Alexia Dug-outs and the Battalion were used in Commutation of the day so far as these enhances were practicable. The Battalion received orders to move in the afternoon to KEMMEL SHELTERS. This move took place about 9 p.m. and were numerous. A number of 13 men arrived and were posted to companies.	
August 2nd	The Battalion rested during the day, and at night half the Battalion were out on various parts of the line improving communication trenches, returning to bivouac about 2 am 3rd August.	
August 3rd	A Field General Court Martial was held under the Presidency of Capt. Potts, for the trial of Pte. G. Maxford for desertion. The C.O., 2nd in Command, all Coy. Commanders, the under E trenches, and T/form went in the position of the line allotted to the Battalion for next period in the trenches. Weather very wet. Orders received to relieve East Surrey Regt. on the morrow.	
August 4th	The Battalion rested during the day	

(73989) W4141—463. 400,000. 9/14. H.&J.Ltd. Forms/C. 2118/10.

WAR DIARY or INTELLIGENCE SUMMARY

Army Form C. 2118.

Hour, Date, Place	Summary of Events and Information	Remarks and references to Appendices
August 4th (Continued)	and paraded at 7-30 p.m. to march out and relieve East Surrey Regt. Orders received to start up until further orders as a mine was to be blown up at 11 p.m. in (Trench 13) one of the trenches we were to relieve. The Battalion stood by until 11.10 p.m. when orders were received to march to LOCRE for the night as relief could not take place. Capp Lackersey CI/GSL went to hospital sick, and it/Lordship assumed the duties of a/capp.	
August 5th	7-15 p.m. and relief carried out successfully about 11-30 p.m. Battalion Head Qrs. went at T. Farm. Battalion reserve at NEWPORT. Coy. in trenches.	Trenches occupied were E1, E2, E3, E4, E6, 15, 15½, 14A, 14B, 14S, ST.P VIII, & ST.P IX.
August 6th	night 5½ & 6½ in trenches guard. At about 7 am. Capt E.G. Young left No 15 trench to observe from a point further in rear and was	

WAR DIARY or INTELLIGENCE SUMMARY

Army Form C. 2118.

Hour, Date, Place	Summary of Events and Information	Remarks and references to Appendices
August 6th (continued)	shot through the neck and killed. About 9.15 a.m. the whole battalion moved to the brow of a gorse plain. The enemy were conveyed there. Shell burst at that time in the village church yard. The men of 88th Battalion were evidently wounded on the fort. A crowd of enemy was killed under the enemy's major Linden-Thomas.	No 6964 Pte. T Crooks were also also wounded & died consequently. It took place about 11p.m. and buried by the side of Capt Henry
August 7th		
August 8th	Weather fine. Orders received that our artillery troops commence a bombardment on the Black Redoubt, and necessary preparations were taken. Battalion commander took up position at Buttic. Head Quarters, but Batt. Staff remain at Colts themQrs ready for movement if necessary.	

Army Form C. 2118.

WAR DIARY
or
INTELLIGENCE SUMMARY.

(Erase heading not required.)

Hour, Date, Place	Summary of Events and Information	Remarks and references to Appendices
August 9th	Bombardment carried out, and Battalion received renewed plan from Division at NEWPORT. Coy. to advance from reserve to extend our line by taking over trenches 43, 46, and SP VIII + SP IX (a). 'B' Coy. were allotted to this line and on relief the relieving company to the Y & E. Brickworks. 'C' Coy a company of the Battalion in front of 'Coy a company to follow 'D' in rear of platoon of 'C' Coy. + the return to D coy.	
August 10th	Received orders — up in above area. ⟨…⟩ to letter at 3-50 p.m.	
August 6th 11th	O/S 14583 Pte R.J. Kempe was killed by a shot in the head whilst firing over the parapet, trying to take orders ⟨…⟩ from Brigade. Held Queries? this body was interred in the REMPLACE Château ground.	

(73989) W4141—463. 400,000. 9/14. H.&J.Ltd. Forms/C. 2118/10.

WAR DIARY or INTELLIGENCE SUMMARY

Army Form C. 2118.

Hour, Date, Place	Summary of Events and Information	Remarks and references to Appendices

August 11th (contd.) — quiet at night.

The Battalion was relieved by the Yorkshire Regt. and B Coy of the Yorkshires being employed at identifying and marking drowned shelter trenches.

August 12th — The Battalion rested during the day and C Coy was supplied with clothing. 230 men were employed digging trenches & communication trenches until about 1.30 am 13th.

The following changes took place among the officers:— Capt Hughes from Transport staff to Command B Coy, Lieut Ardern to Transport officer. Lieut Griffiths from D Coy to C Coy.

August 13th — Spent in trench front of line. Made about 300 yards of trench & other trenches apparently trying to make
on the KEMMEL — WIEPSTRAAT road.

WAR DIARY
or
INTELLIGENCE SUMMARY.
(Erase heading not required.)

Army Form C. 2118.

Hour, Date, Place	Summary of Events and Information	Remarks and references to Appendices
August 14th	Orders received for Battalion to move to OCRE, and to be ready to move by the truck right, move expected not bet 3.30/- night, move put fully dressed at later. OCRE - same Blot's previously occupied in bivouac stage.	Lordship Lieut. A. Gray. 1 Suffolk Regt.

Army Form C. 2118.

WAR DIARY
or
INTELLIGENCE SUMMARY
(Erase heading not required.)

Instructions regarding War Diaries and Intelligence Summaries are contained in F. S. Regs., Part II. and the Staff Manual respectively. Title pages will be prepared in manuscript.

Hour, Date, Place	Summary of Events and Information	Remarks and references to Appendices
August 15th	The Battalion was at Rest in Loere. The weather was fine. Orders were received for 1 machine gun of Battalion to relieve a gun of Welsh Regiment in S.P.8	
August 16th	There were the usual parades during the morning, and in the evening a concert was given by the 28th Divisional Concert Party, and held at the Convent Loere at 6pm and was much appreciated by the troops. Captain Hannay reported sick and was admitted to hospital. 2nd Lt. E. West assumed command of "C" Coy vice Capt. Hannay. The order for the relief of 1 machine gun of the Welsh was cancelled.	
August 17th	The weather was good. Orders were received to relieve the 2nd Cheshire Regiment in the trenches. One officer ten boys was sent to reconnoitre. Captain Hoggan reported sick, and was admitted to hospital. 2nd Lieut Wright assumed Command of "B" Coy vice Captain Hoggan. Orders were received about 10pm that Lord Kitchener	

Army Form C. 2118.

WAR DIARY
or
INTELLIGENCE SUMMARY
(Erase heading not required.)

Instructions regarding War Diaries and Intelligence Summaries are contained in F. S. Regs., Part II. and the Staff Manual respectively. Title pages will be prepared in manuscript.

Hour, Date, Place	Summary of Events and Information	Remarks and references to Appendices
August 17th Cont'd	reviewed by the French War Minister, who so invited the Battalion at SCHERPENBERG at 11.45am on the 18th inst.	
August 18th	A very busy day was spent. The Battalion paraded at 9.30am and proceeded to SCHERPENBERG for Inspection by Lord Kitchener and the French War Minister. The other units present were the 2nd Kings Own Lancashire Regiment and the R.F.A. reserve of 3rd Brigade whose guns were in action but O.I Wood and 100 men were quickly marched to BAILLEUL as a Guard of Honour and proceeded on motor buses. At 11.15am Lord Kitchener arrived and the Staff arrived, and carried out the Inspection. A medal was afterwards presented to a French Staff Interpreter. No speeches were made. Lord Kitchener departed at 11.30am to visit a part of the line. The Corps Commander expressed his appreciation of the general appearance of the 9th Support Regiment. The Battalion marched back to Locre and prepared to go out to the Trenches	

WAR DIARY or INTELLIGENCE SUMMARY

Army Form C. 2118.

Hour, Date, Place	Summary of Events and Information	Remarks and references to Appendices
August 18th Cont'd	The 2nd Btn the Regiment was successfully relieved at 10.47 p.m.	
August 19th	Our Trenches were visited by the Corps Commander, Sir Charles Fergusson who was very pleased with the steadiness of the men, and suggested various improvements and said he hoped that by the time of his next visit, every Company would possess a Periscope Rifle. At present only 5 being at the disposal of the Battalion. The enemy posted up a notice in the trenches to the effect that they had taken KOVNO.	
August 20th	The night was passed very quietly. A draft of 20 NCOs then arrived and joined the Battalion Reserve in NEWPORT, dugouts. No. 8011 Cpl. A.E. Oakley was accidentally wounded with a bomb. The Enemy produced a Captive Balloon during the	

Army Form C. 2118.

WAR DIARY
or
INTELLIGENCE SUMMARY

(Erase heading not required.)

Instructions regarding War Diaries and Intelligence Summaries are contained in F. S. Regs., Part II. and the Staff Manual respectively. Title pages will be prepared in manuscript.

Hour, Date, Place	Summary of Events and Information	Remarks and references to Appendices
August 20th Contd	Nothing in the direction of "Warneton".	
August 21st	Our Snipers were active during the day and were of opinion that they accounted for one or two of the Enemy. No. 19052 Pte. Fridgate A Coy. and No. 18449 Pte. Nicholls "D" Coy were slightly wounded. No. 18345 Pte. Bowles "A" Coy was unfortunately killed. Nothing of great importance occurred during the day.	
August 22nd	The night was fairly active with Rifle fire the firing broke out with a heavy burst, but closed at about 10 a.m. The usual work was carried on during the day, improving the trenches. The Chaplain of the Force arrived at 3.45 p.m. and carried out the Funeral of No. 18345 Pte Bowles. D/Cpt Pte Bowles.	

Army Form C. 2118.

WAR DIARY
or
INTELLIGENCE SUMMARY

(Erase heading not required.)

Instructions regarding War Diaries and Intelligence Summaries are contained in F.S. Regs., Part II. and the Staff Manual respectively. Title pages will be prepared in manuscript.

Hour, Date, Place	Summary of Events and Information	Remarks and references to Appendices
August 23rd	The night passed off quietly. A heavy bombardment was kept onwards at about 4 am the worst hand action was carried on during the day. The Brigadier Genl telephoned a 5th Corps message which stated "the 2nd Batln Suffolk Regiment succeeded in bringing down an enemy aeroplane with Rifle fire at about 4 pm." The enemy showed great activity opposite 14 A Trench by sending over 15 Rifle females, one knew in the trench wounding four men, three were badly knocked about, the fourth only being slightly wounded. A message was sent through to our Artillery who quickly put a stop to the enemy's female morning. The Brigade sent the following message.	

Army Form C. 2118.

WAR DIARY
or
INTELLIGENCE SUMMARY
(Erase heading not required.)

Hour, Date, Place	Summary of Events and Information	Remarks and references to Appendices
August 23rd Cont.	to be issued to the troops :— "The following enemy ships were sunk in the Gulf of RIGA. 1 Super Dreadnought, 2 Cruisers, 7 Torpedo Boats. Enemy attempted a landing in force at TERNAU about 100 miles N. of RIGA All Boats sunk before reaching shore." The above message was received by the troops with great joy and enthusiasm. Seven copies of German Newspapers were handed into E.1 Trench, and forwarded to Bde. H.Q. Ohio	
August 24th.	The night passed off fairly quietly, but about 5 p.m. enemy fired some very heavy shells which dropped about 200 yards from Batt. H/d Ohio apparently searching for our Artillery.	

WAR DIARY or INTELLIGENCE SUMMARY

Army Form C. 2118.

Hour, Date, Place	Summary of Events and Information	Remarks and references to Appendices
August 24th Cont'd	The usual trench duties were carried out during the day. Our Snipers in E1 claim two victims. Patrol of D. Coy from 15 trench went forward before dawn and secured a flag placed in position by the Enemy on the previous night midway between the two lines. A "New" Rifle Grenade of Enemy fell in trench 14 B and did not explode. The Intelligence Officer from the 2nd Batn. H.A. Qrs. came up and extracted detonator, and pronounced the same that it was a most useful specimen. One man of D. Coy was wounded in the left elbow, by gunshot. No. 19457 Pte H. Hawkes. Orders were received that Battalion would be relieved on the night of the 25/26 and march	

WAR DIARY
or
INTELLIGENCE SUMMARY

(Erase heading not required.)

Army Form C. 2118.

Instructions regarding War Diaries and Intelligence Summaries are contained in F. S. Regs., Part II. and the Staff Manual respectively. Title pages will be prepared in manuscript.

Hour, Date, Place	Summary of Events and Information	Remarks and references to Appendices
August 24th Cont^d.	to Kemmel Shelters	
August 25th	The enemy had placed another flag up. to replace the one which was taken from them, this time they tied it to a tree, about 7 or 8 yds from their trench, this flag was also secured by the Battalion, thus making the 2nd flag secured in the trenches. Our machine Guns and Signallers were relieved by the 2nd Cheshire Regiment and proceeded to KEMMEL SHELTERS about 7pm. The Battalion was successfully relieved about 10.30 pm and proceeded to KEMMEL SHELTERS independently, C. Coy bringing the captured flag with them.	

Army Form C. 2118.

WAR DIARY
or
INTELLIGENCE SUMMARY.
(Erase heading not required.)

Hour, Date, Place	Summary of Events and Information	Remarks and references to Appendices
August 26th	The Battalion received orders to furnish working parties to the extent of 450 men to work on VIERSTRAAT and NORTHUMBERLAND FUSILIERS lines. These parties left at 8pm and returned about 2 am 27th inst. Remainder were employed on Inspections, bathing and changing of worn clothing. The Battn furnished all road guards into KEMMEL.	
August 27th	The Battalion again furnished working parties as for the 26th inst. Orders were received that the Battalion would move to LOCRE on the morrow.	
August 28th	The Battalion moved into BADAJOS HUTS. Locre at 3 pm. Orders were received to relieve the 2nd Cheshire Regiment in the trenches on the night of 29/30th.	

Army Form C. 2118.

WAR DIARY
or
INTELLIGENCE SUMMARY.
(Erase heading not required.)

Hour, Date, Place	Summary of Events and Information	Remarks and references to Appendices
August 29th	The Battn attended Divine Service at 10 a.m. and afterwards prepared for proceeding to the trenches. At 6.15pm the Battalion marched off via DRANOUTRE to take over the trenches from the 2nd Cheshire Regiment. The Relief was successfully carried out by 10.37pm and the Battalion Head Quarters was established at T. FARM. No. 8060 Pte Barber was hit on the arm by a Stray shot; a slight wound only.	
August 30th	The night passed off quietly. The artillery exchanged a few shots during the night. No. 19198 Pte Bowens was accidentally wounded, having a finger shot off his left hand, whilst lifting his rifle to a position to take a shot at the Enemy. The trigger caught on corner of a projecting sandbag, it is believed.	

Army Form C. 2118.

WAR DIARY
or
INTELLIGENCE SUMMARY.
(Erase heading not required.)

Instructions regarding War Diaries and Intelligence Summaries are contained in F.S. Regs., Part II. and the Staff Manual respectively. Title pages will be prepared in manuscript.

Hour, Date, Place	Summary of Events and Information	Remarks and references to Appendices
Aug not. 31st	The night passed off fairly quietly, but the weather turned out very wet indeed. The morning opened badly by our losing No: 9145 Pte. Brissett., who was killed whilst on "morning Patrol". Hardly an hour had elapsed before No 19025 Pte. McKeown was killed, being shot through the head whilst firing at the Enemy over the parapet. During the afternoon the Enemy fired about 15 Rifle Grenades into the Trench, severely wounding 2nd Lt Peterman, No. 1706 Cpl. Culley, 8555 Pte harden and slightly wounding No 19391 Pte Marshall. Our artillery opened fire and stopped the Enemy doing any further damage, but unfortunately the first shell fired by our guns was defective and burst short, wounding slightly	

Army Form C. 2118.

WAR DIARY
or
INTELLIGENCE SUMMARY.
(Erase heading not required.)

Instructions regarding War Diaries and Intelligence Summaries are contained in F. S. Regs., Part II. and the Staff Manual respectively. Title pages will be prepared in manuscript.

Hour, Date, Place	Summary of Events and Information	Remarks and references to Appendices
August 30th Contd	No 16905 Pte. Andrews and No 9490. Pte. Brooks. No 15275. Pte. Colthofer. The funeral took place of Pte. Brushett and Pte. Reavon at 3 p.m. at the "Dressing Station Farm." This is unfortunately the most disastrous day spent in the de trenches, up to date.	Lindsay's Lieut. & Adjutant Suffolk Regt

84th Bde.
28th Div.

1st SUFFOLKS

SEPTEMBER

1 9 1 5

On His Majesty's Service.

1st Suffolk Regiment

Army Form C. 2118

A.G'S OFFICE AT THE BASE
3rd. ECHELON. M. E. F.
12 NOV. 1915
CENTRAL
No. M.F.C/

WAR DIARY
or
INTELLIGENCE SUMMARY
(Erase heading not required.)

Instructions regarding War Diaries and Intelligence Summaries are contained in F. S. Regs., Part II. and the Staff Manual respectively. Title Pages will be prepared in manuscript.

Place	Date	Hour	Summary of Events and Information	Remarks and references to Appendices
Sept.	1st		The night passed off quietly about 11.15 am enemy opened fire with heavy Catubi guns, and shells burst in vicinity of S.P.7. One smashed through the officers Dug Out, notably killing 2nd Lieut E. H. Nowell. This unfortunate Officer was dug out from the debris, and buried at the Dressing Station. Farm at 2 p.m. At 5 p.m. our artillery bombarded the "Black Redoubt" and Peckham (2 prominent points held by the enemy). At about 11.15 p.m. a carrying party of "A" Coy. were returning from the trenches and a hot fire was opened on them by the enemy, killing one	

1st Suffolk Regiment

Army Form C. 2118

WAR DIARY
or
INTELLIGENCE SUMMARY
(Erase heading not required.)

Place	Date	Hour	Summary of Events and Information	Remarks and references to Appendices
	September 1st Cont.d		No 18646 Pte Vince and wounding 3 No 18588 Pte Boardman No 17772 Pte Bowers. 18890 Pte Bunn. At about the same time a working party of "C" Coy reported the death of No 18605 Pte Campo in Rear of the trench, shot through the Breast. A report was received from the Field Ambulance 85th Brigade at "Dranoutre", that 2nd Lieut Paterson had died of his wounds, and was buried in Dranoutre Cemetery. at 4.30 p.m. and that Corporal Bailey was progressing favourably. Orders were received that the Bn. was moved the	

1st Suffolk Regiment

Army Form C. 2118

WAR DIARY
or
INTELLIGENCE SUMMARY
(Erase heading not required.)

Instructions regarding War Diaries and Intelligence Summaries are contained in F. S. Regs., Part II. and the Staff Manual respectively. Title Pages will be prepared in manuscript.

Place	Date	Hour	Summary of Events and Information	Remarks and references to Appendices
	September 2nd		relieved on the morrow night, by the 2nd Cheshire Regiment, and moved to "Kennel Shelters" to Bivouac. The Batts was relieved at 10.30 in the evening and marched to Kennel Shelters where they bivouaced for the night. The weather was very wet indeed.	
	September 3rd		Orders were received in the morning for the Batts to move to LOCRE. The Batts moved off at 3:30pm and Billeted in Baarjos Huts LOCRE.	

1875. Wt. W593/826 1,000,000 4/15 J.B.C. & A. A.D.S.S./Forms/C. 2118.

1st Suffolk Regiment

Army Form C. 2118

WAR DIARY
or
INTELLIGENCE SUMMARY
(Erase heading not required.)

Instructions regarding War Diaries and Intelligence Summaries are contained in F.S. Regs., Part II. and the Staff Manual respectively. Title Pages will be prepared in manuscript.

Place	Date	Hour	Summary of Events and Information	Remarks and references to Appendices
	September 4th		The weather was still very wet. The Batt'n aid the usual daily Parades.	
	September 5th		The Batt'n paraded at 10 a.m. for Divine Service, which was held in the open at the back of Badajos Huts. 2nd Lieut West reported sick, and was admitted to Hospital the same day	
	September 6th		Orders were received at 16 p.m. August 5th that the Batt'n were to vacate the Huts at LOCRE at 10 a.m. on the morrow, and proceed to the Shelters at KEMMEL. The Batt'n moved off at 10 a.m. to the	

1st Suffolk Regiment

Army Form C. 2118

WAR DIARY
or
INTELLIGENCE SUMMARY
(Erase heading not required.)

Instructions regarding War Diaries and Intelligence Summaries are contained in F. S. Regs., Part II. and the Staff Manual respectively. Title Pages will be prepared in manuscript.

Place	Date	Hour	Summary of Events and Information	Remarks and references to Appendices
	September 7th		Shelters at Kemmel where they bivouaced. The Batt. rested during the day, and in the evening the Batt. furnished working parties at night to the extent of 450 furnished from all Coy's.	
	8th		Orders were received to take over the trenches held by the 2nd Cheshire Regiment. A Field General Court martial was held at LOCRE. Lieut Smith Captain Wood attended. Prosecutor & members respectively. The Batt'n marched off to trenches Nr T Faryn at 9 pm	
	9th		Weather very fine. There was only 1 casualty. One man wounded.	

WAR DIARY
or
INTELLIGENCE SUMMARY
(Erase heading not required.)

1st Suffolk Regiment

Army Form C. 2118

Instructions regarding War Diaries and Intelligence Summaries are contained in F. S. Regs., Part II. and the Staff Manual respectively. Title Pages will be prepared in manuscript.

Place	Date	Hour	Summary of Events and Information	Remarks and references to Appendices
September	10		"D" bay who were in supports did some fatigue work for the Brigade. Two men were wounded	
	11		Lieut Smith started on short leave for 8 days.	
	12		Capt. O. J. Ward assumed the duties of adjutant. 2nd Lieut Clowson joined the Batn and was taken on the strength.	
	13		Weather was very fine. 2nd Lieut Clowson was posted to "D" Coy. The day passed off very quietly. Orders were received that the Batn. would be relieved on the night of 14/15.	

1st Battn. Suff. Rgt.

Army Form C. 2118

WAR DIARY
or
INTELLIGENCE SUMMARY
(Erase heading not required.)

Instructions regarding War Diaries and Intelligence Summaries are contained in F.S. Regs., Part II. and the Staff Manual respectively. Title Pages will be prepared in manuscript.

Place	Date	Hour	Summary of Events and Information	Remarks and references to Appendices
September 14			2nd Lt Hollowake rejoined. During the day a report came from the trench that a number of cylinders or pipes about 12' by 1' were visible between 1st & 2nd German lines, caused a certain flutter, not only at the Brigade, but also at the Division. The Battn. was relieved in the evening by the 2nd Cheshire Rgt, and Cays marched into Kemmel Shelters independently. Shelters till 2.30.	
	15		The Battn. stayed at Kemmel. Shelters till 2.30. as 2.30. the Battn. moved off to Locre and billeted in Badajos Huts. 2nd Lieut West rejoined	

1/4 Batt. Suffolk Regt.
Army Form C. 2118

WAR DIARY
or
INTELLIGENCE SUMMARY
(Erase heading not required.)

Place	Date	Hour	Summary of Events and Information	Remarks and references to Appendices
September	16		Baths were allotted to the Battn. The whole of the Battn. during the day Bathed and complete sets of clean clothes.	
	17		There was a C.O.S Parade at 11 am. A Field General Court Martial was held at B. H. Qrs. LOIRE. Maj. G. L. Sinclair Thompson was President. Orders were received for the Battn. to move to KENNEL SHELTERS.	
	18		At 2.30 pm the Battn. went to the Shelters and billeted in Bivouacs. The weather was very fine. 2nd Lt. Sippe was transferred to the 1st. Kensingtons. 2nd Lieut Snooks reported sick, and was admitted to Hospital.	

1st Suffolk Regiment

Army Form C. 2118

WAR DIARY
or
INTELLIGENCE SUMMARY
(Erase heading not required.)

Instructions regarding War Diaries and Intelligence Summaries are contained in F.S. Regs., Part II. and the Staff Manual respectively. Title Pages will be prepared in manuscript.

Place	Date	Hour	Summary of Events and Information	Remarks and references to Appendices
	Sept 19th		The Battalion did the usual fatigues during the day.	
	20		The Battalion attended Divine Service at 10 a.m. The Battalion received orders to vacate Kemmel Shelters at 2.30 pm. to make room for the Canadians, the Battn. moved to a farm Nr Kemmel Shelters at 2.30 pm. 2nd Lieut Thomas R.A.M.C. left the Regt and was succeeded by Lt. Webb	
	21		The whole of the Battn. paraded at 8 am and marched off and joined the 84th Brigade at LOCRE, and thence to BORRÉ and went into Billets	

1st Battn. Suffolk Regt.

Army Form C. 2118

WAR DIARY
or
INTELLIGENCE SUMMARY

(Erase heading not required.)

Instructions regarding War Diaries and Intelligence Summaries are contained in F. S. Regs., Part II. and the Staff Manual respectively. Title Pages will be prepared in manuscript.

Place	Date	Hour	Summary of Events and Information	Remarks and references to Appendices
September	22nd		The Battalion paraded and went for a Route march at 9.30 am till 12.30. Starting point the Dressing Station in the following order. B. C. D. A. H.Q. Detachment 12 have fainted.	
	23		The Battn at 9am went for a Route march till 1.30. 2nd Lt Eckington went on short leave. 2nd Lt Wright reported sick, and was admitted to Hospital.	
	24		The Battn paraded at 3pm for a Route march. Orders were received for the Battalion to stand to till 6am on the following morning 25 inst and be ready to move off in an hours notice.	
	25th		The Battalion stood by till 6am.	

1st Suffolk Regiment

Army Form C. 2118

WAR DIARY
or
INTELLIGENCE SUMMARY
(Erase heading not required.)

Place	Date	Hour	Summary of Events and Information	Remarks and references to Appendices
	Sept 26th		Received orders to be ready to move off at 7.45. At 7.45 marched from Bone to LE CORNET MALO with 1½ hours halt south of Frevillers. 30 feet out had rejoined at 8 a.m. Spent night in Bivouac at LE CORNET MALO.	
	September 27th		Left Bivouac at 9 a.m. and embussed and went through Bethune and debussed at BEUVRY continued by motor route to a point a quarter of mile W. of NOYELLES, spent the night in Bivouac.	
	28		At 9 a.m. the Battn. marched to a field Nr. Pr. head qrs. at SAILLY LA BOURSE and bivouacked for the night.	

WAR DIARY
or
INTELLIGENCE SUMMARY
(Erase heading not required.)

1st Suffolk Regiment
Army Form C. 2118

Place	Date	Hour	Summary of Events and Information	Remarks and references to Appendices
Sept. b.	29th		Battalion moved off at 3pm in the direction of CAMBRIN and occupied some reserve trenches. At 6 pm orders were received that Battn was to go to 9th Division Hdqrs took us to VERMELLES where Battn and 10th Line transport halted for the night.	
	30	At 6 am.	Battn moved off and occupied old support trench and CURLY CRESCENT trenches, being in reserve - about 8 hours to move up the C.T. trench. Lieut Inshaw and two men wounded by shell fire	
		At 5.30 pm	we came again under orders of Br. Bde and moved down the Hulloch Road to VERMELLES where we also Battles were filled and Battn. occupied Lancashire Reserve trenches; turned about midnight.	

N.B. Oakes. Captain
Commanding 1st Suff Regt

84th Bde.
28th Div.

Embarked with Bde for Salonika 24.10.15.

1st SUFFOLKS

OCTOBER

1 9 1 5

On His Majesty's Service.

1st Battalion Cuthbert Regiment

Army Form C. 2118

A.G's OFFICE AT THE BASE
3rd. Echelon, M.E.F.
12 NOV. 1915
CENTRAL

WAR DIARY
or
INTELLIGENCE SUMMARY
(Erase heading not required.)

Instructions regarding War Diaries and Intelligence Summaries are contained in F.S. Regs., Part II. and the Staff Manual respectively. Title Pages will be prepared in manuscript.

Place	Date	Hour	Summary of Events and Information	Remarks and references to Appendices
			No. M.F.C.	
October	1st		3 Fatigue parties of 100 men each paraded about 10 am at 5.30 pm 600 of Battn under Lt Col White paraded as an R.E. Party and 2 smaller parties as carrying parties. The R.E. did not arrive, and Battn was ordered to move to support trenches to cover an attack by 1st Welsh and 2nd Cheshires on "Little Willie" by daylight 2nd Oct. The Battn had relieved the Support Trenches, except Lieut. Parsons and crew with 70 "B" Coy who were sent to "Big Willie" for duty with "Northumberland Fusiliers"	
	2nd		about 10 am "Battn Head Qrs. and "A" Coy, moved down to CENTRAL KEEP, "C" and "D" Coys. remained in Support trenches — "B" Coy. moved to a trench No. B de Hd Qrs. at 1pm. Lieut Col White and Major Sinclair Thomson went to Bde Head Qrs, where instructions were given to attack "triple willie" at 8.30 pm. (the Welsh having been driven out). The C.O and 2nd in command returned from	

1st Battalion Suffolk Regiment

Army Form C. 2118

WAR DIARY
or
INTELLIGENCE SUMMARY
(Erase heading not required.)

Place	Date	Hour	Summary of Events and Information	Remarks and references to Appendices
			reconnaissance at 4.30 p.m. Operation Orders issued at 5 p.m. and Coys moved up the Central Bougeau at 7 p.m., but owing to bloack in C.T. could not get into the fire trench opposite "Little Willie". The time was extended till 10.30 p.m. but at that hour Coys were not yet in position and the time was extended to 12 M N. at 11.30 p.m. "A" Coy had only just reached its position in the fire trench — Coy Commanders were called for by Major Sinclair Thomson to receive final instructions — O.C. "D" Coy, 2nd Lieut Gates could not be found in the dark, and 1 hour more was asked for — this was refused by the Brigade Major — Orders were then given by Major Sinclair Thomson to get the men out of the trenches and line up in 2 lines "C" "B" "D" in front line from L to R and covered off by "A" & "B" — O.C. "B" was ordered to take place of "D" Coy whose men were out to be found — "A" Coy moved off before the other Coys	

WAR DIARY or INTELLIGENCE SUMMARY

1st Battalion Suffolk Regiment
Army Form C. 2118

Place	Date	Hour	Summary of Events and Information	Remarks and references to Appendices
	Oct. 4		were ready, and the attack of the other 3 Coys inclined to the right - the attack failed. Casualties 7 Officers and about 150 other ranks. Men were collected in the fire trench and at 4.30 am the Battn. was ordered to attack again - but this order was cancelled. The Battn. was "relieved" by the 85th Brigade at 6 am and moved down to LANCASHIRE Trenches arriving there 11 am. Battn. moved at 12.30 am to support trenches to support S&R Bgde. and moved down at 3 pm to LANCASHIRE Trenches - and remained there for the rest of the night. Lieut Col. White was admitted to Field Ambulance.	
	5		Major G.A.L. Sinclair Thomson assumed command of the Regt. The Battn. marched to ANNEQUIN at 10 am. The Battn. received orders to march to BETHUNE and went into	

1st Battalion Suffolk Regiment
Army Form C. 2118

WAR DIARY
or
INTELLIGENCE SUMMARY
(Erase heading not required.)

Instructions regarding War Diaries and Intelligence Summaries are contained in F. S. Regs., Part II. and the Staff Manual respectively. Title Pages will be prepared in manuscript.

Place	Date	Hour	Summary of Events and Information	Remarks and references to Appendices
October	6		Billets for the night. 2nd hand West resumed the duties of adjutant.	
	7		The Battn. marched off at 8 am to BUSNES and went into Billets for the night Near PERRIERE.	
	8		The Battn. after cleaning up etc. passed the day in rest, finding the usual guards. Drafts were sent in for all deficiencies etc. The Battalion commenced a course of training at 6.30 am. A draft of 60 arrived from the Base. Weather Close.	
	9		A Regular training programme was commenced. Bombers were made up to 200 and instruction with live bombs was commenced.	

1st Battalion Suffolk Regt

Army Form C. 2118

WAR DIARY
or
INTELLIGENCE SUMMARY
(Erase heading not required.)

Instructions regarding War Diaries and Intelligence Summaries are contained in F. S. Regs., Part II. and the Staff Manual respectively. Title Pages will be prepared in manuscript.

Place	Date	Hour	Summary of Events and Information	Remarks and references to Appendices
Oct br	9th		The following officers command Coys:—	
			"A" Coy. 2nd Lt. Prothego.	
			"B" Coy. Lt. Panama with 2nd Lt. Shaw to	
			"C" Coy. 2nd Lt. Owen with 2nd Lt. Kilner	
			D Coy. 2nd Lt. Llewin.	
	10		The usual programme of work was carried out, with Divine service at 9.30 am.	
			Captain Llewellyn W.L. joined the Battalion.	
	11		The day was passed with the usual training programme. The weather continued to be fine.	
	12		The Battn paraded for a Route march. Bathing was commenced at GUARDEBEQUE and shooting on the range.	
			2nd Lt. Kilner went to Reconnoitre New Trenches	

1875 Wt. W593/826 1,000,000 4/15 J.B.C. & A. A.D.S.S./Forms/C. 2118.

Army Form C. 2118

WAR DIARY
or
INTELLIGENCE SUMMARY

1st Battalion Suffolk Regt.

(Erase heading not required.)

Instructions regarding War Diaries and Intelligence Summaries are contained in F. S. Regs., Part II. and the Staff Manual respectively. Title Pages will be prepared in manuscript.

Place	Date	Hour	Summary of Events and Information	Remarks and references to Appendices
October	13th		The remainder of the Battalion finished bathing.	
	14		The Battalion continued with the programme of Training. Weather fine.	
	15		The Battalion paraded at 11.30 am and was inspected by the G.O.C. 28th Division.	
	16		Lieut Col. Thomson was admitted to the Field ambulance.	
	17		Orders were received for the Battn to be ready to move off at 8.30 am in the morning.	
	18		The Battalion paraded at 9.30 am and marched to BETHUNE and billeted at the French Barracks. The Head Quarters were ordered at the RUE DE VICTOR HUGO.	

1st Battalion Suffolk Regt.

Army Form C. 2118

WAR DIARY
or
INTELLIGENCE SUMMARY
(Erase heading not required.)

Instructions regarding War Diaries and Intelligence Summaries are contained in F. S. Regs., Part II. and the Staff Manual respectively. Title Pages will be prepared in manuscript.

Place	Date	Hour	Summary of Events and Information	Remarks and references to Appendices
od.	18th		Orders were received for the Battalion to be ready to move off at an hours notice on the morrow from 9 am.	
	19th		2nd Lieut proceeded to ROUEN for a month, and Captain M L Llewellyn assumed the Duties of adjutant. The Battn stood by during the day. A course of training was continued during the day. 2nd Lieut Fielding joined the Battn and was taken on the strength and posted to "D" Coy.	
	20		The Battn stood by. till 9 am. Training was continued throughout the day.	
	21		The Battn received orders in the morning to entrain at FOUQUEREUIL FORGUES at 3 pm. and marched off at 12.45 pm and entrained for MARSEILLES.	

Army Form C. 2118

WAR DIARY
or
INTELLIGENCE SUMMARY

(Erase heading not required.)

1st Battalion Suffolk Regt.

Instructions regarding War Diaries and Intelligence Summaries are contained in F.S. Regs., Part II. and the Staff Manual respectively. Title Pages will be prepared in manuscript.

Place	Date	Hour	Summary of Events and Information	Remarks and references to Appendices
Oban	21st		The entrainment was carried out satisfactorily, and the Battalion proceeded to MARSEILLES. Major Hon. H.E. Joicey joined, and took over "Command"	
	22nd		} In the train.	
	23rd			
	24th		Arrived at MARSEILLES. Rations were served out and the Battalion marched to the point of embarkation, and proceeded to ALEXANDRIA on the H.T. "Huronia". The transport officer and 38 men proceeded by the H.T. "Shropshire". Captain A.J. Campbell joined, and took over the duties of adjutant, and Capt. R.M.B. Needham the duties of senior major	

1875 Wt. W593/826 1,000,000 4/15 J.B.C. & A. A.D.S.S./Forms/C. 2118.

Army Form C. 2118

WAR DIARY
or
INTELLIGENCE SUMMARY

(Erase heading not required.)

1st Battalion Suffolk Regt

Instructions regarding War Diaries and Intelligence Summaries are contained in F.S. Regs., Part II. and the Staff Manual respectively. Title Pages will be prepared in manuscript.

Place	Date	Hour	Summary of Events and Information	Remarks and references to Appendices
October	24th		Captain Llewellyn took over the command of "A" Coy.	
	25		2nd Lieut. E. Lemon was transferred to "D" Coy.	
	26		on the A.T. "Ivernia"	
	27		on the A.T. Ivernia	
	28		on the A.T. Ivernia	
	29		on the A.T. Ivernia	

Army Form C. 2118

WAR DIARY
or
INTELLIGENCE SUMMARY

(Erase heading not required.)

Place	Date	Hour	Summary of Events and Information	Remarks and references to Appendices
Oct	30th		Disembarked at ALEXANDRIA, and proceeded to MARMOURAH Camp, by train, under canvas, weather very hot.	
	31st		The Battalion paraded for Divine Service at 4.15 pm.	
			The Battalion paraded in the morning for practicing the attack.	

W. Campbell, Captain
Adjutant
1st Battalion Suffolk Regiment